Joe Swi

Quadrille

JOE'S
urban
garden
handbook

Editorial Director **Jane O'Shea**
Creative Director **Helen Lewis**
Designer **Mary Evans**
Project Editor **Laura Herring**
Picture Research **Nadine Bazar,
Samantha Rolfe**
Production Director **Vincent Smith**
Production Controller **Ruth Deary**

First published in 2008 by
Quadrille Publishing Limited
Alhambra House
27–31 Charing Cross Road
London WC2H 0LS
www.quadrille.co.uk

This paperback edition published in 2009

Cataloguing in Publication Data: a
catalogue record for this book is
available from the British Library.

ISBN: 978 184400 837 7

Printed in China

contents

INTRODUCTION

Do you have a small urban garden? A yard, roof terrace or even a balcony? Do you want to transform it into an exciting, contemporary space so that you can invite friends over, or simply so that you have somewhere to escape to after a hard day's work?

City dwellers often pay a premium for a property with a garden, so that they can have access to their own highly prized 'private outside space'. They have great intentions of developing it so that they can spend as much time as possible outside. Very quickly, however, most people become disillusioned, claiming that "it's too much work", "it's overlooked" or "the kids have made it all muddy". Their negative feelings lead to their garden becoming increasingly ignored and neglected. And so it continues across the city. Looking out of the window from the North London Line train, I see hundreds of these forgotten plots. Some look as though their lawns may get mown once in a while out of a sense of duty, but many are completely abandoned. They are hardly interesting, exciting outdoor spaces that you would want to spend any time in. What a huge waste of space!

Any outdoor space in an urban environment, however small, is an invaluable bonus and these days creating a fabulous outdoor plot need not require you to develop horticultural expertise. Getting stuck in every now and then can be great fun and may even lead to a passionate interest. It is when the demands become greater than you can cope with that the garden begins to be a chore. Then, your garden will quickly start to look messy, you become embarrassed and frustrated with the whole damned thing and eventually stop caring. Why do so many of us feel that we should tackle our gardens from start to finish ourselves, and that if we don't then we are somehow shirking and letting ourselves down? Keen gardeners can get unbelievably snooty and some would even go as far as to say that you don't deserve to have a good garden if you can't do it all yourself! In my opinion, this is absolute rubbish. I enjoy eating good food, but I'm not a great cook. Does that mean I shouldn't be able to eat what I want because I can't cook it? Of course not! Personally, I'm a huge gardening lover and enjoy both the physical exercise involved and all the creative challenges. I do, however, appreciate that not everyone is going to get the gardening bug, but that doesn't mean that they can't enjoy having a great garden.

Whether you're looking to employ a professional at certain stages along the way or are going to have a go at it yourself, a successful garden will need focus, a little inspiration, an initial input of time and energy and, let's be honest, money. You might think that you'll just grow a few plants in some yoghurt pots and rope in a builder friend to landscape your garden over the weekend in exchange for a few cups of tea. Sure, it can be done very cheaply, but I've seen few successful gardens built this way. It's time to get real. It's important to be careful that any money you do put into your garden is invested wisely. It's all too easy to spend your hard-earned cash on the wrong things, such as buying large specimens of fast-growing perennials that may look good from day one, but will need dividing up within a couple of years. You'd be far better off with a fabulous sculptural specimen tree, which will hold a small garden together all by itself.

You'll certainly need to get your head round budgets, but if you're canny, the initial outlay should be repaid immediately by adding value to the property. You will probably need to employ an expert to assist with the more technical and structural issues, and if you feel really overwhelmed by design and planting then enlist the help of someone with a little knowledge – even if it's just to get you started. Why not? You would do the same for your plumbing or a new kitchen layout, so why not with the garden?

Many people find choosing the right plants for their garden rather daunting. In fact, the plants are the most flexible part of the job. They are generally quite forgiving and can usually be lifted, moved around, pruned and even chopped up and composted to go back into your garden. Of course, I appreciate no one wants to waste their money, but everyone will make a few mistakes to start with. Not even professional garden designers expect to make real gardens look amazing instantly; those ones are just for the shows. A real garden takes time to develop and will need the occasional blitz and jazzing up to keep it looking fresh, but these should come into the fun category rather than the chores.

The physical act of gardening is all about getting outside, connecting with nature and your environment, de-stressing and being creative; in my view there are no downsides to it. Like most things, however, you need to get started just by starting, and then you'll at least have something to work from to take it to the next stage – even if it's just a cleared patch of bare soil or an idea sketched on the back of an envelope. Rather than trying to tackle everything in one go, instantly visualising your dream, I find the best designs are built from layers of key decisions. Design is a process rather than just a magical happening, so the earlier you start and the more you engage in the process, the more you will get out of it and the better your chances are of finding the right solutions. There are, of course, a million different design solutions for the same plot, but the aim of designing your own garden is to create an outdoor space that is entirely personal to you, and in which you feel completely relaxed and comfortable.

Inspiration can come from all sorts of places. Visiting other gardens will fill you with ideas for possible layouts and planting, even if the visit only helps you to decide what you definitely do not want to include in your space. Local gardens will also show you which plants thrive in your immediate area. But look beyond existing gardens, as ideas are generated by many other influences: art, public landscapes, architecture and product design can all trigger valuable ideas and help to stimulate interesting designs.

Developing your ideas and vision for your garden is an exciting process, but be realistic and practical in your approach. I have seen too many gardens that, on first appearance, seem to be very 'clever', with an instant wow factor, but that completely ignore the most important factor of all: time. Time will ultimately prove whether a garden is sustainable, practical and can last the distance without looking dated.

All of us are increasingly aware of our environment, and how the future of the planet is intrinsically linked to our current lifestyle. The urban garden has an important part to play here. City gardens actually contain a wider range of biodiversity than many rural gardens and most farmland areas. Back-to-back gardens act as wildlife 'corridors', enabling easy movement and providing diverse habitats for insects, birds and mammals. To encourage this biodiversity we need to be more relaxed with our approach to gardening, which suits me down to the ground as that's the kind of character I am! But overgrown wildlife havens do not make for great usable city spaces; it's all down to getting the balance right and making space for nature.

Green spaces help to cool our cities considerably, which is becoming a big issue for all of us. Plant transpiration (where water evaporates from the leaves) has the effect of cooling the surrounding air, in a similar way to the effect of perspiration. Increasing the proportion of green space – through developing our gardens, parks and green roofs – to hardscape, such as architecture, paving and roads, can help to reduce urban temperatures by several degrees. Lack of water is also likely to become a huge issue in the future and, of course, our gardens and plants rely on water. A sustainable garden should not need constant watering from the mains supply to keep inappropriate plants alive. Choosing the right plants, taking time to ensure good soil preparation, composting, installing water butts and being able to 'harvest' and store any rainwater which falls on your house, garage, shed and paving areas are all ways to make your garden more sustainable. With the mass construction of new homes and the ongoing major upgrades and refurbishment of older houses there are now fantastic opportunities to include greener practices in our homes and gardens. We all need to keep on our toes for any such openings and, wherever possible, pressure architects and property developers not to neglect the garden space, as it is far too often seen as an afterthought with regard to both design and budget.

Too many city children have become detached from outdoor life and the urban garden is the perfect place for them to reconnect with nature from an early age. Kids get so much out of gardens and gardening, and, although it's not always easy to make a small garden all-inclusive, it should certainly have enough in it to encourage them to use it whenever possible. The enclosed back garden is a safe place to play, but it should also be a social place where children can interact with each other away from their parents' prying eyes. Family gardens shouldn't be too sterile either, while ensuring that safety is paramount; there's a big different between those that I would call 'educational' plants, such as the prickly holly, which, once grabbed, will not be touched again for a while, and the downright dangerous ones, like a spiky yucca.

Whatever your style and whatever you intend to use your garden for, a well-designed outdoor space is the perfect antidote to modern urban life. As well as directly benefiting the homeowner on a day-to-day level, the combined volume of these areas means so much for everyone who lives in and visits the city. They are uplifting spaces that are full of life, which provide nourishment for your soul. I simply couldn't live in London without mine. If you have a forgotten garden then I hope this book inspires you and helps you to get out there and reclaim it for all of us.

LIFE'S TOO SHORT

time for a rethink

Keen gardeners understand that patience is an important part of gardening life; we have to wait for as long as it takes to achieve results. The reality for most of us, however – especially if we live in the city – is that we move properties more frequently than ever before, and most of us simply can't, and don't want to, wait an eternity for a great garden. Maybe we have inherited a garden that doesn't really work for us or, perhaps, it just about functions and has some good parts, but we don't like it enough to want to live with it forever. So, why wait? Life's too short!

The way we look at and use our gardens has changed dramatically over recent years. Although mature, well-considered planting will certainly help to make a good garden great, an urban garden these days is reliant on many other elements beyond the flora. Whether you're moving into a new property or have been looking at the same tired old garden for far too long, there comes a time when you need to be ruthless. There are many factors to consider – some of them emotional, some practical and plenty of them economic. Believe me, you've got to get tough if you want to achieve good results. This is certainly not the time to let your emotions get in the way – like planning your entire garden around an overgrown rose bush that you inherited with the house from a little old lady!

You need to be focussed and clear about what you really want – and what you will be able to realistically achieve within your existing space, time and budget. The key points to assess are any major positive aspects of the garden – as well as any negatives – and what can be done about them. Every item needs to be considered in regard to whether it adds any value to your garden and whether it is possible to incorporate it into the masterplan.

There are no set ways of approaching a rethink. But, whether you're looking at a completely new design, changing a certain area or simply reshaping the lawn, it is, as with most things, worth doing as much research as possible beforehand in order to find a way forward that you're comfortable with. You will also need to decide whether it's going to be a DIY or DFY (Done For You) garden – or a combination of the two – perhaps getting help with a design and the hard landscaping, but choosing to plant up the garden yourself.

Designing and building your own garden is an extremely satisfying experience. But you must be aware of your own capabilities. In the long run, employing a professional garden designer and/or someone to help with the construction may be the best decision you could ever make, saving a lot of cost and heartache. And, unless money's no object, being in tight control of the budget is fundamental to seeing the project through, and ensuring that the garden actually gets completed.

To save money, go with the site's existing levels.
The precise placing of major retaining walls in a
split-level garden can make or break the budget. Unless
it is well thought through it can involve huge quantities
of spoil to be either excavated or brought in as infill.

As you assess your site walk into every corner and look around in all directions. The main sight lines from inside the house are vital, but also consider how the house will look when in you are in the garden looking back towards it and whether it can be softened with planting. Plants such as these box balls are extremely useful for formalising areas, and will thrive in both sun and shade, whereas the olive trees and alliums need a sunny spot.

assessing existing pros and cons

After years in the business I can walk into a garden and immediately assess its pros and cons, work out what's worth keeping *in situ*, what's worth moving around on site and what should be immediately removed. The experience comes from seeing hundreds of gardens and providing unique design solutions to budget. If possible, try to view your own garden with the same professional and unemotional confidence.

The majority of urban gardens are small and it is, therefore, pretty easy to observe all the key points of the site with regard to its size, shape, aspect, existing boundaries, slopes and existing soil conditions. These all form the vital framework of your garden and have to be respected, whether or not they can be changed.

To start with, disregard everything else within the garden, as all the smaller elements — such as the planting, paving, sheds, washing lines and lawns — can either be moved around or removed completely if they don't add anything to the garden.

SIZE AND SHAPE

Look at the overall size and shape of the garden. Is it long and thin? Is it a standard rectangle? Or is it a more awkward shape, such as a triangle or rhomboid, without any of its boundaries square to each other? Odd-shaped gardens are often viewed as being problematic, but I like the way that they already have an identity, which can give a garden its own unique sense of place. It's a good idea to put the survey down onto paper, as you'll be able to see the interaction of the boundaries or any awkward angles, and so be able to make sense of them far more easily.

Walk around the garden so that you cover every square centimetre and keep looking in every direction, including up and down, as you move about to explore what you see from every point in it. Stand on walls, look over fences, squat down as if you're sitting. You may look like a bit of a loony, but you'll get a lot out of it! Don't expect to come up with an instant design on the spot. This exercise will help you to see your garden with new eyes and will give you clues as to where you feel overlooked, which parts feel squeezed or claustrophobic and how you can make the best use of level areas in the garden to save on shifting earth.

YOUR GARDEN'S ASPECT
The aspect of your garden is the way that it faces – north, south, east or west. This, when combined with the effect of any trees, shrubs or structures that overshadow it, will define the amount of sunlight each area receives throughout the year. If you have lived in the same house for several years then you will be at a huge advantage, as you will be familiar with the movement of the sun – how high it gets in mid-summer and how low it is in the winter. Track it over a few days and make a note of the sunny and shady areas at different times of the day.

EXISTING SLOPES AND LEVEL CHANGES
It's well worth measuring the overall slope across the entire garden. Use a couple of sticks stuck into the ground and run a taut piece of string between them. Use a spirit level to make sure that it is precisely level. Then, measure down from the string on each stick to the lowest point. Compare the two to find out the difference in height. This will give you an idea of how many steps or level changes you will need to get from A to B if the whole garden is to be accessible.
(Also see Box of Tricks, pages 78 – 9)

SOIL
Dig a few test holes around the garden to get an idea of where the good and poor areas of soil are. Leave the holes until it rains heavily (or pour a bucket or two of water into them) to see how quickly the soil drains, or whether it holds on to water.
(Also see Box of Tricks, page 61)

DRAW A SITE ANALYSIS
Measure the site and sketch out a brief site analysis. Make a note of any areas of poor soil, the sunny and shady spots, where you feel secluded, where you feel particularly exposed to onlooking neighbours and any areas that are particularly difficult to maintain, such as sloping soil that might spill onto paving areas. Some key decisions, such as where to place the seating area, where's best to grow herbs etc. can be established from this analysis and will form the basis for the next stage of the design.

The positioning of seating areas and the overall flexibility of the space are more important in small urban gardens. This roof terrace has been designed to draw you away from the house and closer to the boundary, where the seating area is more secluded.

existing structures

Painting the existing walls white links them with the new structures. The layout has been kept open for a spacious feel in what could easily be a dark, claustrophobic area.

Existing structures have often cost either yourself or the previous homeowner a lot of money to install. Depending on whether they have been fixed in place permanently, it may be possible to work them into the redesign by leaving them where they are, repositioning them in a better spot or updating them to work with the new design and materials.

WALLING AND OTHER BOUNDARIES

Boundaries are essential for marking out a property's perimeter and for providing some security and privacy. If any work does need to be done on them, it should be done first, so that other areas aren't trampled on at a later stage. Walls are expensive to rebuild, but if they are leaning, wobbling and downright dangerous then there are no short cuts and no choice but to make them safe. It may be possible to build piers every few metres to increase stability, rather than instigate a complete rebuild. Or, if the damage is superficial, it may simply be a case of repointing where necessary. If in any doubt, get a structural engineer to advise you. Fences can be tested by pushing and pulling on them. Remedial work may be possible on an old fence, such as replacing the odd post or panel that has rotted, but if on its last legs it is worth considering replacing the whole length. If, however, the fence is structurally sound, but you think it unattractive, there are simple ways of losing it visually within the design. *(See Box of Tricks, page 68−9)*

SHEDS AND SUMMER HOUSES

Buildings such as sheds and summer houses can sometimes be moved, but don't count on it as they will often collapse when dismantled. If they are small and structurally sound they can usually be relocated in one clean lift onto a new base, but you will need plenty of strong people for the manoeuvre. Bigger buildings that have been built *in situ* may be useful for storage, but can be overly dominant visually, and eat up valuable garden space. In my experience, these are the hardest structures to remove and often need industrial breaking equipment. If there is a possibility that asbestos was used in its construction you must inform the local authorities and have them remove it, which can get expensive.

PERGOLAS AND TRELLISING

Hand-crafted arches, pergolas and trellising are often beautifully built, giving your garden a degree of identity. They *can* be moved, but it is usually not an easy task. The big decision is whether or not they will work with your future garden style. They can dominate a city garden and often are traditional in their style, so consider if that will work with your masterplan.

PONDS

Existing ponds usually go one of two ways: they are either poorly maintained, smelly things stuck in a corner of the garden with half the liner showing, or they are serious constructions managed by a koi fish expert with pumps and filters all over the place. Although ponds are great for wildlife and you may have inherited a goldfish or two, or even some frogs and newts, they are also dangerous if you have young children around. Any existing wildlife can be safely rehoused in rent-free temporary accommodation (in water-filled dustbins and buckets!) if you are looking to build a new pond, otherwise be sure to help them find another permanent home. *(Also see Stress Busting, pages 120−1)*

PAVING

Areas of well-laid paving can probably be incorporated into your design if they are of a finish that you like, and they can be reshaped or cut along the edges. Expensive materials, such as Yorkstone or slate paving, can be lifted, cleaned and reused, but make sure that you either have sufficient quantities for your new design or can buy exactly the same material to bulk up the quantity. The sub base is very rarely reusable and will almost certainly have to be excavated out.

LIGHTING AND POWER SUPPLIES

Old lighting systems very rarely attain current safety standards and will need to be replaced by a qualified electrician.

existing planting

Many gardening books will recommend that you live with your garden for a year, so that you can see what comes up in terms of bulbs and herbaceous perennials, and also so that you can understand how the sun works its way around the garden. Well, in an ideal world that's certainly a good idea, especially if you've inherited the garden from a keen gardener, but it will make it a rather slow process. I find that you can usually work out the main plants in your garden, and I definitely wouldn't recommend redesigning your garden around any perennials or bulbs, which can easily be lifted and moved if you do decide to keep them.

Trees and shrubs are, however, another story. They are essential to most gardens for the sheer volume that they add, as well as the cover that they provide and the wildlife they draw in. The characteristics of any existing mature trees should be carefully considered; a garden will immediately have more substance if at least some mature planting is kept. For example, a healthy but gnarled magnolia tree will instantly give the garden a feeling of permanence. If it is overgrown or an odd shape or is too dense with branches it can probably be pruned, or the canopy can be lifted so that you can walk under the tree. Seek advice from a qualified tree surgeon about pruning it into a decent shape. If, however, it's a poorly looking tree with badly damaged bark it may not be worth keeping and incorporating into your new design.

Self-seeded trees, such as sycamores and ash, and also large conifers which were once planted as a hedge but have now outgrown their space will definitely need to be cut back. First, check with your local council to find out whether you are in a conservation area and, therefore, have to abide by local laws, or whether there is a Tree Preservation Order on any particular tree before you undertake any tree surgery.

Mature hedges, such as yew or box, will hopefully be in the right place, as they are certainly worth keeping if at all possible. They respond well to cutting back hard and can be reconditioned back into shape, or perhaps you might consider trimming them into a new funkier shape to work with your new garden.

If you have a small tree that has only recently been planted, it's possible that it could be moved to a new position. Deciduous and evergreen shrubs – even large ones – can be lifted and moved, as long as it is done at the right time of year. Ideally, move deciduous shrubs in the late autumn and evergreens in early spring. Make sure that you dig up as big a rootball as possible to move with it. If you damage any of the roots in the process, don't worry, just cut them off cleanly with secateurs before replanting, to avoid any risk of infection. All large shrubs will benefit from having some of their top growth cut back at the same time.

Perennials are generally fast growing and if you are planning on keeping any in your garden, then they can usually be potted up or 'heeled into' a planting area of the garden temporarily, whilst any construction work is carried out. Just make sure that you keep them well watered.

Ornamental grasses prefer to be moved in spring rather than the autumn. Plan well ahead if you are looking to move any ground-grown plants, as it should be done during dormant periods. They are almost impossible to keep alive if moved during the hot summer months, and even if they do survive they will take ages to recover fully and will look below par until they do.

The large eucalyptus tree in the neighbouring garden forms
an important part of the garden's composition and increases
the sense of space. Consider all plants and trees – both in
your garden and those nearby – and whether the extended
landscape enhances or detracts from your garden.

budgeting

The size of any trees, in this case the multi-stemmed silver birch, will also have a bearing on cost, but it is worth the investment for instant effect.

People like to work their budgets in different ways. Some like to start with a fixed total that they don't want to (or can't) go over, whilst others have more financial flexibility and like to get a 'feel' for how much a garden costs, weighing up what they want against what they will get for their money, and then making a judgement on whether the investment is worth it to them or not.

City dwellers are becoming more and more aware of how a great garden can significantly add economic value to their property, often far more than it actually costs them to implement. It'll also make a house easier to sell when the time comes. And, like a fine wine, the more it matures, the better it gets!

Many projects go way over budget or fall short of the owners' expectations, through a lack of understanding of the total price of their garden. Usually this is due to unrealistic costing of every single element that goes into it. It's not just materials and plants – which may have been seen 'on sale' in the local garden centre – that form the total figure. City gardens do tend to cost more due to parking costs, skip licences, poor access and materials' permits when storing in the street etc. It all adds up!

All the possible costs that need to be considered and budgeted for:
● The site survey
● Consultation, design, specification and possible project management/overseeing
● Structural engineer for any complex or major construction work
● Site clearance including taking the debris away (skip hire etc.)
● Site infrastructure works, such as drainage, services and relocation of manholes etc.
● Hard landscaping (materials and labour)
● Soil preparation
● Soft landscaping (including turf, plants and labour)
● Accessories such as lighting, irrigation, sheds, furniture, water features etc.

Break your budget down into all these sub-sections, even for small projects, so that you can make sure that you have every angle covered, even though some may not be relevant. Also make sure that the VAT is accounted for with any quotes because it is unlikely that this will be recoverable, and it is a common mistake to leave this out when dealing with professional quotes.

Once you have done a little initial research you can start to fill in your list with budget costings for each section. You can also include the details of possible professionals that you might enlist to undertake each role at this stage. Sometimes it's a bit of a chicken-and-egg situation, as you won't know what many of the elements will cost until you have a finalised design.

Some companies will design and build your garden for you, whereas many designers will undertake the site survey, the design and the planting and will project manage the construction, which will be done by someone else. Just make sure that you're the one who's in control of the final budget, and ask as many questions as you need to feel comfortable.

STAGING WORKS
Large projects can have their work staged over a year or more in order to spread out any expenditure, whilst still aiming for a high-end garden. This can work well, ultimately leading to a fully completed, impressive garden, but it can, however, also increase the overall costs, as landscape contractors will usually charge more to leave and return to a site rather than running the job through in one hit.

CONTINGENCY
It doesn't matter in how much detail you plan, there will always be discrepancies and unforeseen problems when designing and building a garden. These could include issues such as underground drainage works, slower periods due to poor weather or a delivery charge that has been omitted. A contingency of between five and ten per cent of the overall figure should be put to one side and made available if necessary.

employing a garden designer

It is well worth getting an experienced, fully qualified garden designer involved at some level, as their job is to get the most out of your space on the budget you have available. You may find it hard, but be completely open and honest about money and discuss budgets from the initial contact to avoid any confusion. Research garden designers and how they work, as many have different processes and degrees of involvement. Also look at their websites for an idea of their level of experience, and at their portfolio for a flavour of their house style, if they have one. Remember that professionalism should rank way higher than whether you like their personality or not.

BRIEFING
To get the most out of any garden designer you will need to brief them properly. They will probably have their own system established, in order to ask all the right questions, but if you feel they've missed anything out, even small but important things such as where to put the washing line, then don't hold back!

INITIAL CONSULTATION
Some designers charge for an initial consultation and some don't. Others may charge you a fee, which will then be discounted if you decide to engage them further. Paying a full rate means that you will want value for money, and the designer is more likely to give you firm ideas on that initial visit. In a free consultation, although you won't have lost anything, the designer will be pitching for work and may be less open to coming up with immediate ideas.

SKETCH MEETING
Designers are increasingly incorporating a sketch meeting into a paid initial consultation. This is where they will come up with some instant thoughts on layouts and ideas for planting. It can be a really productive way to move the project forward and to give you food for thought, whether you are looking to design your garden yourself or are going to engage them further. Be clear about your intentions at the outset and ask whether you get to keep the sketches, and, if so, who will own the copyright.

LAYOUT, PLANTING AND SPECIFICATION
If you want a complete professional redesign then you will need a full set of drawings. Some designers will undertake their own site survey if it's pretty straightforward, but for large or complex sites you'll need a detailed site survey in CAD (Computer Aided Design) form. Some designers will charge for this by the hour, and others as a percentage of the job. Find out exactly what you will get regarding concepts, details, specifications etc. and whether there are implications if you require a re-draw – if you don't like the scheme or it's over budget.

TENDERING PROCESS
Once you have a design in mind you will need to start getting prices for the work. A designer can oversee this process for you and will often recommend landscapers that they have worked with before and with whom they have a good understanding, which is especially important on complex builds. The designer needs to write a detailed specification, so that each of the companies tendering is pricing for exactly the same garden – with the same finishes, depth of foundations etc. This also forms part of their contract. Make sure that everything is covered and check whether it is an estimate or a quote, which are two entirely different things. The cheapest quote may not always be your best bet and if it's significantly lower than the others, then be wary. When considering tenders find out details such as when the contractor can start the work, how long they expect it to take, how many people will be on site, their payment structure, whether they use subcontractors and whether they have a code of conduct. Professional companies will be able to tell you this.

A professional garden designer will focus in on the main elements of the garden brief and tie them together with confidence, to create a strong look. These large hornbeam trees do a great job of creating a backdrop and increasing privacy.

PROJECT MANAGEMENT AND SOURCING

Most designers will oversee the project and help to source plants for you, charging either a percentage of the overall price or an hourly rate. Some good landscaping firms may have this element built into their price, and if the design is simple then this can be kept to a minimum. There will, however, inevitably be issues from time to time, and these need to be resolved quickly so as not to delay the work.

CONTRACTURAL STUFF

I know it's boring, but every single decision needs to be documented. Read any contracts with designers and landscapers carefully and make sure that they have the correct insurance cover. Any verbal changes or decisions to install extras that are made on site during a build *must* be written down to avoid any confusion over payments at the end.

DESIGN AND BUILD

Some landscape companies have in-house designers who work closely with the landscapers to come up with a simplified solution. Many new companies, such as Modular Garden, which I co-founded and am Design Director of, work on a complete design-and-build basis. They analyse the available budget and come up with a design and installation solution based on the brief that was set by the client during the initial consultation.

having a go yourself

Gardeners learn quickly from their mistakes. Designing and building your own garden from scratch and doing a poor job isn't, however, like cooking a meal that doesn't taste good and knowing not to make the same mistakes again: the stakes are far higher; there's often only one hit at it. Don't feel that you have to do the whole project yourself from start to finish. My advice is to get experts in at certain times to do the work that you either can't do yourself to a high enough standard through a lack of skills or physical demands, or simply don't have time for. A hybrid solution is usually the best way forward.

DESIGN

Having a good initial design will make or break your garden. If you have a flair for design or know precisely what you want, then why not have a go at it yourself and see how far down the design line you get? And possibly surprise yourself. After all, your own time will probably be the only free cost in the whole project. Even if you end up turning to a professional designer you will have really focussed on your needs, so no time will have been wasted. Measure the site up accurately to scale and play around with basic shapes for areas to see how they might fit together.

SITE CLEARANCE

Once you have a fixed design, the clearance may only involve removing excess vegetation from the site. It is more likely, though, to need some removal of hard surfaces, too, such as paving and the sub base. It might also require some re-levelling. This is pure physical work, both in bagging up the excess and taking it through the house, or barrowing it directly to a skip. If you're fit enough, then give it a go. The final levels before construction are important, so make sure that you don't over or under excavate, as a landscaper will have to adjust any discrepancies.

CONSTRUCTION

Putting down a timber edge for a new lawn or laying a landscape fabric requires fairly basic skills, so you can probably do these yourself. If you have some carpentry skills, then decking is a good DIY project. When it comes to the digging and laying of foundations, building steps and walls and laying down paving, the professionals may make it look easy, but to get a high-quality finish and to ensure that all the drainage falls the right way takes practice. There are also on-site health and safety issues, and guarantees of the works by a professional, a guarantee you can't give your own handiwork.

PLANTING

I think that planting is the most enjoyable of all the gardening jobs, as you instantly make a connection with the plants you're putting in and begin to understand how they grow. If you are a complete novice and you've had help in designing the planting scheme, this is where you can get more involved. Lay out all the plants on-site first, trying to space them according to their future spread. Plan two or three years ahead for perennials and longer term for trees and shrubs. Keep standing back and looking at the distances between them, trying to imagine how they will grow together and tweak them around until you're happy. Even the most precisely scaled planting plan will be altered once the plants arrive and every professional designer will move them around accordingly. And don't worry about it: if you still get it a bit wrong — if they grow too quickly or too slowly — they can usually be moved later on.

MAINTENANCE

A garden is never static and a little ongoing maintenance will ensure that your garden fulfils its potential. Most tasks are simple and fun, and if the garden is designed correctly will work for whatever time you have available. (See Blitzing, pages 158–169)

The advantage of having a small urban garden is that you can transform it quickly with limited materials and resources. Remember, though, that if you're aiming for a slick modern look, the detailing and finishing will make or break it.

fencing
Off-the-peg fences are fairly easy to construct if you have basic carpentry skills. Make sure that you use a spirit level to get them perfectly plumb. And, rather than putting all the posts up at once, place a single post in the ground and fix each panel as you go along for a tight fit.

decking and steps
Decking large level areas is relatively easy, but integrating steps, making sure that all the risers and treads are even and safe, needs detailed calculation. When contemplating facing existing steps with decking for a new look, think about hiding the sub frame and consider how the water will drain.

dense planting
Planting up a small garden where all the planting areas are relatively contained is an easy and fun part of the job. Look for plants that will thrive in the specific setting and choose ones that will serve a particular role, such as adding height or a particular colour or texture where you want it.

BONES

creating your garden's framework

The bones of a garden are its permanent layout and infrastructure, over which the more transient elements – such as seasonal planting, styling and furniture – can be layered. The way the different areas link together and flow into each other creates the garden's framework. It should be an enticing yet functional space with the potential for seasonal adjustments and it should never feel forced.

Fundamental to a garden's success is achieving a good design layout. This chapter looks at case studies of a variety of city gardens and analyses how and why they have been designed and what their triumphs are. There are many tried and tested ideas and basic principles shown here that can be adapted easily for your own plot. Plagiarism is all part and parcel of designing a garden, so don't hold back if you see something that you like and that you think will work particularly well in your own city space. The common theme running through all the case studies I've chosen to include is confidence. Although they are all very different in their style, none of these gardens come across as confused or bitty. When a garden layout tries to answer too many questions at once, incorporating lots of different elements, it often loses its clarity and becomes diluted and weak. These examples have all kept true to their aim without distraction. They also show that by carefully considering scale and proportion, the whole space becomes more organised and feels a lot more generous. Many garden designers have an individual style and will have favourite combinations of plants, materials and detailing, but a good designer will always keep an open mind and rarely impose personal tastes over substance, just to make a statement. How a garden is seen from inside the house is also very important. Many city gardens make use of the windows and doors as starting points to establish a grid across the plot. This will create a strong, geometric look that will not only give your garden a contemporary feel, but the clean lines will also keep down your budget for cutting and shaping materials.

Gardens have always been about a desire to dominate and organise nature and impose ourselves onto the land. The city garden invites us to take this principle on board, and often encourages us to go a stage further, to create an outside space far removed from any rural reference. In fact, a city garden will look less contrived and sit more comfortably in an urban setting if it searches closer to home for its references – the architecture surrounding it, its extended views and any modern materials found in the metropolis, such as steel and concrete, as well as glass, stone and timber.

Water, whether it's a pond, rill or feature, tends to sit far more comfortably in a garden when it has been integrated during the design layout stage. This is a simple, yet extremely effective waterfall built of steel and left to go rusty.

A FAMILY GARDEN

Historically, a traditional family garden would have had an extremely simple layout with a main lawn area, perhaps a swing or sandpit and some tough plants that could cope with a football or two being kicked around. Nowadays, family demands on the city garden are greater than ever. We all want to use the space to relax, entertain, work and play, but also as a place to create a wildlife haven, so that our environmentally aware children can come into contact with the engaging biodiversity of the city. Of course we also want it to look great, work as an extension to the house and be as low maintenance as possible! Maybe we're asking too much, but I believe that with good planning and clever design it is possible to make an interesting, exciting space that works on different levels for everyone to enjoy.

Plot size: 5m x 15m.

decking stepping stones
Diagonally placed decking stepping stones through the planting area have been laid so that they can't be seen from the house. They rise a little towards the back to help deal with the small slope and there is low planting in-between.

planting combinations
This generous planting area separates the spaces, but also helps it feel like a lush, fully planted garden. The soft evergreen mounds of *Hebe topiaria* dotted throughout give the garden some structure and the grasses and perennials add shots of seasonal colour and lighter textures.

seating
Comfortable seating is far more inviting than hard wooden or plastic furniture without cushions. Although built-in benches can work well in tiny spaces, non-fixed seating, like this, can be placed in a variety of arrangements, or moved out of the way.

rear deck area
The deck at the back is a great place for the kids to play and hang out in. It makes good use of the overall space and gives the garden direction, being somewhere to go. It's also large enough to double up as a secluded dining area for parties.

raised pond
Water can add so much interest to a garden that has limited space, but it must be installed and maintained to a high standard. This raised pond is teeming with wildlife and the children love to feed the fish and pond-dip with their friends.

hard surface
This natural slate paving is extremely hard wearing. Laying it in a grid adds a contemporary, unfussy feel to the garden. The low retaining wall and pond are finished in the same material to give continuity throughout and help link the areas together.

view from inside

Many houses are being converted to include large glass doors that open out onto the garden. The view from inside the house has, therefore, become more important. Planting nearer the house will increase the depth of the view.

A family garden needs to be designed with flexibility in mind. Of course, the smaller the garden is, the less you will be able to fit in it. If you divide a small garden up too much it can become overly fussy and impractical, and very small areas will increase feelings of claustrophobia. So, rather than trying to squeeze everything in, ensure that the areas you do have are generously sized. Imagine you're a child and think about how you would use, see and move through the garden. My kids go to the local park to play football and ride their bikes, whereas they can climb, swing, garden, draw, play, observe nature etc. in our garden at home – and do at every opportunity. When putting the structure of the garden in place, remember that it doesn't have to be a complete playground and should work for both adults and children alike. Also, children grow up quickly and will want to do different things in it over time, so it needs to be adaptable.

Although a lawn is the obvious choice for a family garden, and cheap to put down initially, there's no doubt that the smaller it is the more impractical it becomes to both maintain and use. In the winter, a small lawn will very quickly become a mud bath and the garden a no-go zone. My garden has hard surfaces – a combination of slate and decking – making it 100 per cent useable all year round, and I don't have to shout at the kids for ruining the lawn or coming in the house covered in mud!

All successful gardens use height, through planting and/or structures, to create interest at and above eye level. I built a simple scaffold-pole pergola over the large deck at the back to add height, but also to hang the tyre swings on – and the kids love to climb up and chat to the neighbours' children. In the summer, the deck is screened from the house with tall plants, making this their own private area. If I had young children I'd keep the planting lower, but I feel it's important for kids to have their own space where they don't feel like they're being watched all the time. When they get older I'll grow plants over the pergola and make it a shady seating area.

play-frame
This play-frame was built
into the deck sub-structure
using galvanised scaffold
poles, which can be cut to
any size and fit together
like grown-up Meccano!
We hung a couple of old
tyres on it for the children
to swing on.

slate blackboard
The slate paving doubles
up as a drawing board.
We have our own in-house
artist, as my daughter loves
to get the chalks out. She
can draw away happily,
knowing that the rain will
wash it all away and she
can start again.

my hideaway
This garden is designed to
be used whenever possible.
The back deck area, which
is mainly the children's
territory, can also become
a lovely secluded shady
spot for me to grab a few
quiet minutes to myself!

work, rest and play

decking bridges
These decking boards run flush with the main paving, helping to break up what would otherwise be a large expanse of stone. Running them through as bridges links together the areas and also provides access to maintain the planting along the wall.

water rill
This is a bold water rill, linking the whole of the garden together lengthways. It has two waterfalls, which, when running, add sound and movement to the garden, but when the pump is turned off the still water brings a contrasting calm mood to the space.

stone steps
When building steps into a garden, you will need to consider how they will work with the proportion and scale of the rest of the garden. Also think about whether your choice of materials will complement the look of your garden, helping to create a cohesive look.

see-through panels
Balustrades are, of course, an essential safety element for any balcony, but they can disrupt a view, or the wrong choice of materials can jar with the rest of the design. Advances in glass technology mean that they can now be built without frames, helping to visually link levels together.

CANAL GARDEN

The success of a garden relies on the choice of materials and planting and the way that they are combined to create an original space with its own identity and character. This design has taken on board the only existing element of real value in the garden – the beautiful boundary wall built from old bricks – but it has updated the very guts of the garden. The strong, geometric design makes good sense of the space and brings a formality to the garden. It also addresses many of the more negative issues associated with urban gardens – shade and awkward levels, for example – turning them into positive aspects.

Plot size: 5.5m x 14m.

box planters
Clipped box has been used since Roman times to help formalise gardens and create the idea of tidiness and control. These square planters with their square box plants introduce simple planting to the raised balcony, helping to reinforce the garden's strong geometry all year round.

getting the tone right

direction of materials
By laying decking widthways across the garden in wide bands you can increase the feeling of space, as this slows the eye as it looks down the garden. There is a fluid rhythm running through this garden, linked by the horizontal joints of the brickwork, through the decking, to the timber screens above the walls.

This garden is a good example of how to effectively combine different materials so that they complement and relate to each other, in terms of their sizes, proportions and finishes. This is, in fact, a shady space – like so many city gardens are – due to overhanging trees and tall buildings close by, but it certainly doesn't feel like it. Its success is down to the fact that everything has been chosen with a particular tone in mind, to keep the garden light and airy and, therefore, inviting and upbeat all year round.

Far too many urban gardens are built from materials that are readily available or easily affordable, rather than first considering what's

bespoke bench
This simple bench sits seamlessly within the design. Its rendered block plinth is painted the same colour as the stone used in the garden, and the timber top is made from the same timber that has been used for the decking. The almost invisible glass back means that you can lean against it, with a cushion or two, but the long view is left open.

the long view
The rill running along the length of the garden maximises the long view, whilst the steps' risers and treads, constructed from the same stone as the rill and paving, ensure that the eye is not distracted on its way.

right for the space. They often become dark, dingy places, which do little to lift the spirits, especially during the winter months, when light levels are low. Expanses of black soil or muddy lawn sap the light and will drain the very life from the garden if you're not careful.

Throughout history we have been obsessed with using colour in our gardens. But many contemporary designers are now aware of the importance of working with tone, and prioritise it, often sacrificing vibrant colour as a result. Look at these images with your eyes half shut and you will see that it is the light stone paving and bleached-out deck that lifts the garden and

bounces the light around, creating opportunities for the plants to add in the darker elements, with plenty of lush green foliage.

The planting has been kept classy and simple with a carefully selected palette of amelanchiers, *Trachelospermum*, *Prunus lusitanica*, and the wonderful green *Hydrangea* 'Annabelle', which looks so comfortable when it can do its own thing and doesn't have to compete for attention with demanding, showier flowers. Many shade-loving plants have glossy foliage – an adaptation developed to maximise their use of limited light in their native setting. Tap into characteristics like this to create strong, sustainable planting.

MODERN TWIST

A modern house demands a modern
approach to its garden. Many people living
in older properties in urban areas are
updating and developing their living space
to work alongside and reflect their more
flexible lifestyles, and the same goes for
their gardens. With developments in glass
and insulation technology, the backs of
houses are now being completely knocked
through and new extensions added on,
which, in turn, open up the garden,
reconnecting it to the house in a new
way and often leading to its rebirth. This
garden has been designed to be viewed
from the back of the house on all floor
levels. The interlocking arcs and circles of
the surfaces run into the verticals, helping
to forge an original and unique identity.

Plot size: 5m x 15m.

curved decking
The almond-shaped deck laid level with the slate paving
ties all the shapes in this garden together. The lines of the
boards run at an angle to the house, but are parallel to the
smaller deck area and the lines of the paving. If they all ran
in different directions it would lose its simple rhythm.

a living roof
Rather than a grim asphalt roof, the artist's studio has a sedum roof, which helps to soften and integrate it into the garden space. Sedum matting is extremely drought tolerant, flowers in spring and will encourage wildlife into a city garden.

curved seating
The reconstituted limestone wall, steps and seat were poured on site, using a complex shuttering technique, but you could build something similar by rendering and painting a block wall. It is the perfect seating height throughout, meaning that, with a few cushions, this garden can easily accommodate plenty of people for a party.

mysterious water
Reflective water without any aquatic planting adds mystery and intrigue, but it must permanently be kept clean to stop it detracting from the overall effect of the garden. The water in this pond is pumped through a filter by a submersible pump in the water, hidden by the overhanging deck.

planting areas
As the planting space is limited in this garden, these tree ferns have been selected for their strong visual impact, particularly when viewed from above – a major consideration in this garden. The curved wall defines the unusual-shaped planting area and helps to lose the straight lines of the existing boundaries.

timber wall
This feature timber wall is made from posts that have been individually concreted into the ground, leaving a small space between each one. It cuts a dynamic and flowing line through the garden, linking everything together, with a view to leading the eye away from its otherwise rectangular shape.

features and styling
This timber wall is a main feature of the garden. As well as breaking up the garden, it doubles up as a back to the bench and its added height creates a strong backdrop to the garden as a whole. Cushions and containers help to style the garden, softening the harder elements and making it a more comfortable place. These need to work with and help lift the design, rather then just looking 'plonked' in afterwards.

artist's studio
This bespoke artist's studio was built *in situ* to work within the garden layout. The journey to work becomes a short walk through the garden, and on a warm day the front of the studio slides open to let the garden in. Wireless Internet allows it to be used as an office as well. Any buildings or structures need to be carefully and accurately designed to fit in with the garden's overall style and layout.

bold, bespoke design

Many modern gardens are designed with the intention of blurring the lines between the interior and exterior spaces, making use of a wide view from inside – from behind a sheet-glass window or through an open door. This garden was, however, specifically designed to do the opposite – to make the garden feel like a very separate place – so that you are conscious of moving from one space into the other and then back again.

The lines of the decking and paving have been laid at an opposing angle to the interior wooden floor to help achieve this separation, but also to draw the eye diagonally across to the furthest corner of the garden where the in-built seating is, maximising the long view from the house. This design technique also means that any walls or planting areas that cut into the garden are viewed obliquely, rather than square-on or straight down the line, making the most of the three-dimensional experience of walking through the garden.

The interlocking curves of the different areas are all carefully considered: confident arcs flowing together, rather than hand-drawn wiggly lines. Clean lines and flowing geometry are what make this a strong garden.

This garden works especially well because, as you walk into it, there is plenty of height and interest at eye level – very important in a small garden. Although the main central area is kept clear for flexibility of use, there's the artist's studio, the timber wall and the height provided by the choice of planting – such as the bamboos in pots near the house and the trees 'borrowed' from the next garden – which work together from the ground up to create several layers of visual interest.

A design like this needs to be executed extremely accurately, and the construction work is probably a little bit tricky for even the most enthusiastic amateur to complete without a bit of professional help. Remember, too, that a design based around curves will always work out to be far more expensive than one formed from straight lines – sometimes up to 50 per cent more – due to the wastage in materials, the extra time and tools required for cutting, and the setting-out of a design like this on the ground before installation.

MODERN CLASSIC

4

Through crisp, stylish, yet restrained design, this garden brings together all the essential requirements for a modern classic city garden. Generous blocks of hard and soft landscaping divide and organise the space both for interest and ease of maintenance, whilst at the same time creating a fabulous and uncluttered garden for relaxing and entertaining. The use of simple geometry, combined with carefully chosen materials and plants, gives this garden a sense of permanence and longevity – vital if a contemporary garden isn't to feel quickly outdated. The planting palette is pared down to avoid looking fussy and to work with the garden's architecture.

Plot size: 15m x 15m.

seasonal planting
The sculptural, multi-stemmed *Cornus* dotted throughout help to link the entire garden together and add all-important height. Here, the brave, black fence really shows them off and the mass underplanting of soft grass creates a textural contrast.

water effects
For the best reflections in a pond use a black liner. This pond has pebbles placed on the bottom to introduce an extra, almost subconscious, visual element.

decking
This hardwood deck area mirrors the gravel and introduces another natural element into the garden. Hardwood timber can be left to turn silver or oiled regularly to maintain its natural colour. When building a deck, consider the drainage beneath.

gravel
Fine compacted or self-binding gravels, like the ones used in French *petanque* or *boule* courts, are becoming increasingly popular in domestic gardens. Although trickier than gravel to lay and needing maintenance they are still fairly economical.

box hedging
This graphic, dynamic hedge is a wonderful use of box, the most classic of plants. It is often associated with formal gardens, but is perfect for an urban space as it adds evergreen structure and will grow happily in partial shade.

visible furniture
When introducing furniture, make sure that it adds to the garden visually when it is not being used. This simple timber bench works well within the style of the garden and provides some direction by adding an inviting and secluded spot to sit and read.

simplicity through repetition

stone finishes
The bridge over the pond, near to the house, turns the walk into the garden into a small journey of discovery. The feature wall, defining the pond's limits, is built from the same stone as the bridge and paving, but has a rough finish to define it as a vertical element in the garden.

To create a garden like this you need to be extremely disciplined. Although it's not strictly minimal, its success certainly relies on what is left out as much as what is put in.

Sure, the results are very impressive, but are you the sort of person who can restrain yourself and suppress the urge to buy a trolley-load of plants and pots from the garden centre just to add a 'splash of colour' in the spring? Those sorts of impulse buys are absolutely fatal to this look. It's the repetition and simplicity of both the materials and plants that work together to create the powerful, yet tranquil, mood of this garden. If you can focus yourself

compatible seating
This seating looks as though it has been custom made for the space, picking up on the horizontal lines of the blinds inside the house. Actually, it is a very carefully chosen off-the-peg product.

statement fencing
Painting an existing fence black and leaving it free from climbers is a daring thing to do, but look how it intensifies and brings out the greens of the planting in front. The dark backdrop also helps to define the contrasting textures of the box balls and the grasses.

and be single-minded enough, then you can create a garden that will hit you on an emotional level, and transport you far away the minute you set foot in it.

Though the plant palette has been pared down to an absolute minimum, this garden is far from boring, as it works well with each season, through the careful selection of plants. The sculptural, multi-stemmed Chinese dogwood, *Cornus kousa* var. *chinensis*, is the sort of tree that really earns its keep in a city garden. It adds plenty of height, creating a ceiling to the garden, and also increasing privacy from over-looking neighbours. In late

spring it is covered in showy, flower-like bracts, and it has lovely, light, fresh green leaves throughout the summer months. In the autumn it produces a beautiful textured strawberry-like fruit, which looks stunning alongside its crimson-purple foliage.

The two blocks of planting on either side of the main path are good examples of succession planting, as they contain masses of the giant early-spring-flowering snowflake, *Leucojum*, which is followed by the alliums in late spring and then the grasses, which stay right through the winter to create an all-year-round sustainable cycle.

disguising fencing
New homes often come with dodgy orange fences! They will age and turn a silver colour over time, but strategically planting climbers, shrubs and trees to obscure the wood will help to lose the imposing rectangular feel that they bring to the garden, and make it seem much larger.

planting combination
This is an eclectic mix of plants: architectural evergreens underplanted with perennials, to pack all the planting spaces available. This can work extremely well in a small garden, as it will create plenty of drama in the planting, with plenty of opportunities to bring in seasonal colour.

raised levels
These deck platforms have been floated above the sloping garden to avoid the need for visually jarring and often pricey steps. The decks are also free-draining, so that rain water can go straight back into the water table, rather than being lost down the drains – an issue we are all concerned about today.

hidden bins

The need to conceal the bins before the weekly collection is a common city refuse problem. Rather than building a permanent screen for them, a couple of well-placed bamboos have been planted for a far softer and cheaper solution. They also create a great backdrop to the garden.

block walls

Rendered and painted block walls are a way of introducing a clean look and permanent colour into a small garden. With the addition of a few cushions they will quickly double up as seating. Make sure that they are easily accessible, without having to tread on any plants.

mini lawn

This mini boxed lawn is a contemporary way of introducing a flat plane of lush green, to keep the overall proportion of hard-to-soft landscaping well balanced. It will require the occasional cut, but you could use scented chamomile or thyme for a similar effect.

SIMPLE STYLE

5

Exciting, well-designed city gardens don't have to cost the earth. The choice of materials, size of plants and any skilled labour you need all combine to form your budget, whether you decide to DIY or get someone in. But, before launching into it, the most important thing to get right is a layout that works for you. This design has converted a standard, boring rectangular space into a dynamic and interesting, yet practical and efficient garden. It incorporates simple flow and movement from the house, rising slightly through the garden to the rear social seating area, and it looks great from all angles as you move through it. It was designed and built on a limited budget for a busy couple who want to spend as much time as they can outdoors and be able to invite friends over, but who don't have loads of spare time to maintain it.

Plot size: 5.2m x 9.9m.

soften it up

Large expanses of surface in a small garden can look too harsh. Rather than laying a solid area of deck, consider constructing a series of independent frames. This will work particularly well over level changes. Don't space the boards too tightly, as the gaps will allow for some low-level planting in the central areas of the garden.

The traditional layout of the rectangular garden with planting all around the perimeter is long gone, as it's often an impractical, uninviting and plain dull solution. These days everyone wants an outside space that works for them, rather than them having to work hard for it. With good design and planning this is now very easily achievable.

I think smaller gardens need more initial consideration than larger ones. A common mistake is to try and make the most of the space by cramming it with 'features', such as pots and water fountains. This garden works well because it is tied together simply through the continuity of materials, and relies heavily on its plants for extra interest, height, colour, texture and scent.

Decking has its critics and is sometimes seen as a 'fad' material, but, in the right situation, it can look classic and there are too many pros to overlook: it's quiet, warm, cost effective and easy to install, without the need for expensive excavation or sub-base work.

net curtains

Your first view of the garden, as you enter it from the house, is very important. Tall, wispy planting in the foreground will create instant interest and increase the desire to explore further. Tall grasses, combined with the self-supporting and long-flowering *Verbena bonariensis* are perfect for this. This sort of planting also works well in front of ground-level windows that overlook the garden.

lawn in a box

This ornamental lawn is packed full of crocus for a stunning shot of colour in the spring. The frame has been made from the same timber as the decking for continuity, with a slate shale edging. Although the lawn is the highest maintenance part of the whole garden, a hand-pushed mower can be quickly run over it, as it is laid proud of the surround.

can you build it?

If you are good at woodwork, consider installing your own deck. You could even build some walls or seating out of the same decking timber, like the storage seat near to the house. Rendered block walls, however, will probably need a specialist to build. The view back to the house shows how versatile the free-draining deck is, as the finished level is tucked just under the threshold.

affordable and achievable

water fountain

This tall rendered and painted block wall forms a clean backdrop to the garden. The wall is also used to raise the source of the water up to a prominent height before it falls into the pond, so that it can be be viewed easily from most areas of the garden.

planting

This is a modern interpretation of the classic mixed border, combining architectural shrubs, herbs and perennials. These all thrive in an open aspect with well-drained soil, and this raised planting area offers both. They are packed together closely to create a full look and to minimise weeding.

raised levels

Raised planting areas are a great way to create visual interest, as they bring the plants closer to eye level, where they are most needed, in what would otherwise be a completely flat garden. The walls double up as seating, so there is plenty of space for people to sit if you're having a party.

hidden storage

A standard shed can be a real eyesore in a stylish garden, but here's a great way to lose it, visually, at ground level. The wall blocks the view whilst still providing easy access and, when the bamboos behind the wall have matured, you'll never even know that the shed's there.

gravel and pebbles

Aggregate, such as gravel or pebbles, can work on many levels when you are designing a garden. It adds texture, and helps keep the composition light. It's also one of the cheapest ways of covering the ground and, with a landscape fabric laid underneath, will reduce weeding to zero.

proportion

The central decking walkway is exactly the same width as the pond and it gives this garden a positive, confident direction, drawing the eye up to the central water wall. The accuracy of the levels is important here, as the deck edge retains the gravel and stops it spilling over.

6

LINEAR GARDEN

There is a lovely rhythm to this design, as it works its way from the house through the central, mainly planted, raised areas, to a great destination of cooling water and a simple seat towards the end. It is a garden that has been carefully designed to look good and to hold interest from all angles. The generously sized areas and a choice of places to sit increase the feeling of space. There is plenty of formality here, with the central path, pond and water fountain all lining up along the central axis, but there is also another, simpler diagonal movement flowing across the space. These two directional layers working together give this garden depth and make you want to move through it and experience it.

Plot size: 5.5m x 30m.

light and dark

The smooth flat planes of the light-coloured walls make the perfect foil for the darker planting in front, such as the dissected purple-leafed maple. The ever-changing light and shadows across the walls also bring life and movement to the garden and its dominant dark reflection adds a certain mystery to the pond.

hard and soft

Harsh lines and strong architecture can be softened as much or as little as you wish with clever planting. This extremely soft, tactile lamb's ear (*Stachys byzantina*) is a favourite with children and wildlife alike and it loves this garden's sunny, well-drained conditions.

practical and low maintenance

This is an extremely practical, low maintenance garden, but it just goes to show that these days the tag 'low maintenance' certainly doesn't have to mean boring.

The design is efficient in its use of space and is relatively simple to build, apart from the pond and waterfall (the implementation of any form of water creates problems, believe me!). The layout is made up from generous interlocking rectangles, which could easily be adapted to work in a smaller or larger plot of roughly the same shape. As well as the basic layout, it has been considered, visually, from the ground up and has three very distinctive layers: the ground surfaces, the low walls creating raised planting, and the taller walls and boundaries. These layers give the garden real volume and height – essential elements in any three-dimensional outdoor design that will be walked through.

The colours of the rendered walls complement and pick up on the subtle colours of the planting, which includes plenty of Mediterranean plants with their silver and grey-green foliage. As well as many of them having delicious, strongly aromatic foliage, they also help give this garden its particular 'holiday feel' – triggered by the sunny, open aspect of the site. Another bonus is that most of the plants are drought-tolerant

meaning that, once established, they will need
little or no watering – an increasing concern.

This would be an easy garden to maintain.
The raised planters are at a comfortable height
to cut back perennials or do a spot of weeding,
there are no fussy planting areas that are hard
to access or which will annoyingly collect leaves,
and the whole garden can be swept easily. To keep
the workload down the choice of plants is vital,
too; there are no plants that need mollycoddling
or regular staking, and, of course, there is no
lawn either. In this garden, a lawn would need
more maintenance over a year than the rest of
the garden put together.

seating height
When you view a garden from
seating height it will appear
very different from when it is
walked through. Raised planters
will increase feelings of privacy
and seclusion when sitting
down, and will also emphasise
the division of areas, even in
a relatively open garden.
When choosing plants for
raised planters consider their
particular shape and growing
habits and whether they might
spill over or sit on the edges
of walls to break up the lines.

BOX OF TRICKS

make your garden work for you

Getting the best out of your site and making your budget work for you are key to successful garden design. The best solutions effectively combine aesthetics with the practical demands of the garden, to create a bespoke and original space that meets all your expectations.

Various techniques will come into play during the design process. Your layout will be driven by a combination of visual demands, such as hiding an ugly wall, and more practical considerations like where to position the bins. You will probably also have to address some more negative aspects, individual to your garden – for example, turning an impractical, sloping site into a usable, desirable space. I'm a firm believer in turning negatives into positives, even when working within a restricted budget and on a tricky site.

Many garden owners, however, tend to become fixated on certain issues – often the negative ones – and, in turn, overcomplicate them and their solutions. This means that they can miss out on the absolute basics of what they are trying to achieve. Look to pare down your design solution to its bare minimum. It will always feel less cluttered and will introduce a classic, long-lasting design, which is often far easier to look after.

Space in an urban garden is usually going to be limited, meaning that every square centimetre will need to work hard. There are tricks to make your garden feel bigger and there are also clever ways of designing some elements into it. Perhaps think about incorporating some concealed storage, rather than just plonking in a shed afterwards, which may not fit with your design or be the best use of space.

There are a several short cuts that you can use to great effect, such as cladding a wall so that it sits aesthetically in your scheme, rather than rebuilding it from scratch. Mostly, however, it's best not to cut corners and for some factors, such as soil preparation, there are few short cuts. They simply have to be done to the highest possible standard, even if it takes time, otherwise the garden won't reach its full potential long-term.

Every garden will need a degree of ongoing maintenance, but, rather than being a slave to it, make it work for you. Before embarking on redesigning your garden, ask yourself exactly how and by whom it will be looked after. Do you have an hour a week, an hour every fortnight, or an hour a month? Be completely honest with yourself, as you will never be able to relax and enjoy your garden properly if every time you go into it you feel as though you should get down to work. Through a good initial design and by taking advantage of the increasing range of time-saving devices, you will find that any work you do put in will be enjoyable and rewarding.

When executed to a high standard, the blurring of
the interior and exterior space works wonderfully
in an urban setting. As well as bringing the garden
inside, it also relates any strong architecture
within the garden back to the building.

left **This is an extremely low-maintenance garden. There is landscape fabric under all the slate shale areas to minimise weeding and a leaky hose irrigation system to water all the planting. The irrigation ensures strong healthy growth, especially to the fastigiated hornbeams, and it will be lost visually when the ground cover, *Pachysandra terminalis*, puts on growth.**

below **The choice and density of planting will reduce the amount of work a garden needs. Make sure to plant up all the areas of bare soil. Here, the combinations of heuchera, Astelia and box create strong textural impact whilst ensuring that any weeds will struggle to get a hold.**

time-saving devices

City gardens have the advantage of usually being small. Yes, I see it as an advantage, as it means that you can take control and dictate precisely how much time you want to spend looking after it. There are ways of seriously cutting back on the amount of work needed without the garden suffering as a result, and it's perfectly achievable to have a great garden without having to weed, water and mow it every week.

IRRIGATION

You'll also be amazed at your plants' rate of growth if they are watered regularly, rather than struggling to survive! Irrigation systems are now affordable, discreet and can easily be installed as a straightforward DIY job.

They make use of a tap computer to provide precise control over when the water will turn on and off and even how much is administered, to ensure proper watering, even when you are away or on holiday. Drip feeds can be individually controlled, so that each plant receives the optimum amount of water, which is, in fact, far more efficient and saves more water than watering by hand. Pop-up sprinklers for lawns are a whole different matter. They are far more expensive, as you'll need a large outside tank for storing the water, rather than running it directly off the mains. The best time to set the water to switch on is the early morning. This means that the plants won't sit being wet throughout the night, which can encourage fungal diseases.

WATER RETAINING GEL

This comes in granular form and, when used sparingly and mixed in with soil or compost, helps to keep your plants moist by absorbing and retaining up to 400 times their weight in water. This makes them ideal for plants that are grown in containers and hanging baskets. They can also be used when planting trees and shrubs permanently into dry areas of the garden, such as under existing trees, against walls or in the eaves of roofs.

LANDSCAPE FABRICS

A landscaping fabric is another must if you are looking to cut down on the work needed to maintain your garden. It will prevent the weeds from coming up, but let water through to the roots of plants. Placed over the soil they can be 'spot' planted, by cutting a hole in the fabric, planting and then mulching over and concealing with pebbles, crushed shells or bark chippings. It works most effectively when planted with shrubs or large perennials, but is no good at all if you are looking to let the plants self seed, or there's a possibility that you might want to add in some bulbs. Make sure to hook the fabric into the earth using thick pieces of galvanised wire that have been bent into a U-shape – if the fabric starts to poke through the mulch it can look extremely unsightly. Use over larger areas of soil as it can be fiddly to lay in small quantities.

PRESSURE WASHERS

A pressure washer may not be the first tool you buy, but consider hiring one every now and then (maybe with your neighbours) as it will speed up the cleaning of everything in your garden, except your plants of course! I clean decks, paving, pots and furniture with one, without the need of chemicals.

DENSE PLANTING

Large areas of bare soil not only sap the light, look dull and are a wasted opportunity, but they also encourage weeds into the garden. Plant areas of soil up densely with ground cover plants to set off other larger plants and you will reduce your workload significantly.

QUALITY TOOLS

Investing in the best and most appropriate tools will make gardening jobs significantly easier, turning them into a pleasure. (See page 60)

GOOD SOIL PREPARATION

Get this right initially and you will save yourself a great deal of time in the long run. (See page 61)

LOW COST

If there is a downpipe running from the roof to a drain in your garden, then you can easily attach an adapter and water butt to it, which will capture and store the rainwater that runs off. This may be enough water for your needs, but it is usually essential to install a garden tap, too. This should be a fairly straightforward job, especially if you have water pipes towards the back of the house, but it may be a bit trickier if you need one at the front.

MEDIUM COST

If you already have an outside tap then look at installing a simple irrigation system. A T-junction attachment, connected to the tap, will let you set up a leaky hose, but you'll still be able to use the main tap as needed. The leaky hose can be run through planting areas, concentrating on the plants that need it most, and joined together with solid lengths of hosepipe where water isn't needed. It can either be slightly buried or mulched over to hide it from view.

HIGH COST

Where money is less of a restriction, you could employ an irrigation professional to install a programmable watering system with personalised fittings. These can be set up to meet your plants' individual requirements, including container planting. There are some DIY systems that are pretty easy to install, too, but they do take a bit of initial adjustment to get just right. Whichever you choose, remember to turn the system off during the winter months.

tooled up

Buying the right tools for the job will make life easier and save you money in the long run. Of course, you'll need to know precisely what tools you'll need, which will depend on the type of garden you have: if you don't have a lawn you won't need a lawnmower! Buying cheap tools is a false economy, whereas well-maintained good quality tools are more efficient, can last a lifetime and are a joy to use.

Forks and spades Those made from stainless steel with wooden handles are the best, as they tend to be lighter, cut through the soil more easily and don't hold on to wet clay. They are also simple to keep clean and the handle can be replaced if it gets broken. The blade and neck should be made from the same piece of forged steel. Check for a balanced weight and a handle that you are comfortable with before buying, and choose either regular or smaller border forks and spades – or both – depending on the job and whichever you're happier using. Keep the spade sharp with a sharpening stone.

Trowel and hand fork Used for hand weeding and planting small plants and bulbs. There's a wide range of shapes and sizes available, but look for a pair you feel comfortable using. I particularly like a long, sharp thin-bladed hand trowel to dig out deep roots of perennial weeds and to plant bulbs in between other plants.

Rake There are different rakes for different needs. A lightweight leaf rake made from heavy-duty plastic is best for leaves on lawns, soil or even paving surfaces, whereas a wire or spring-tine rake can do the same job, but is also for lawn scarification. A soil rake is only used to level and refine soil areas, which may not be an ongoing job in a small garden.

Broom A stiff lightweight yard or deck broom is the best. Look for one with a smallish head that can easily be manoeuvred in tight spaces.

Watering can Metal is more durable, but heavier than plastic. Look for the largest can you can carry easily when full, to save you from having to go back and forth. A free-flowing, easy-to-pour 'rose' is the most important part.

Secateurs There are many different designs and price points for secateurs, including specialist ones for left-handers. The cleanness of the cut is all important, so that any wound will heal over cleanly and, therefore, stop the risk of any disease creeping in. I prefer bypass secateurs, which cut like a pair of scissors, rather than anvil secateurs, which cut down against a flat surface.

Multi-change kits Some manufacturers now make kits with different 'heads' – such as a hoe, rake and broom – which can be attached to a single handle. They can be extremely space-saving and are the perfect choice for the 'occasional' gardener. If you opt for this set-up it's important to buy the best quality that you can afford because the joints and fixing mechanism will get more wear than conventional garden tools.

EXTRAS

Trugs These are really useful for gathering up debris or filling with compost for when you need to distribute it around the garden.
Pruners Long-armed pruners will give you more power to cut through thicker wood and will, obviously, reach further than secateurs.
Ladder A lightweight aluminium ladder is always useful for when it comes time to prune, train climbers or clear the gutters.
Hose An invaluable addition to your garden, and they can be placed out of the way using wall hangings near the tap.
Wheelbarrow Essential for the larger garden to save carrying heavy items around.

soil preparation

Fundamental to the success of any garden is the quality of its soil, and its preparation is certainly not one of those jobs to deal with retrospectively. Although some plants love sandy soil that doesn't retain moisture and nutrients well, and others thrive in boggy, heavy soil, most of the garden plants we grow prefer a good-quality, high-nutrient, well-drained loamy soil. Good soil means that your plants will grow quicker, be far healthier and, in turn, will look better, flower for longer and be strong enough to fend off diseases and pests. A loamy soil with plenty of organic matter mixed into it will retain moisture and nutrients and therefore reduce the need for watering and feeding.

A SIMPLE TEST
Grab handfuls of moist soil from different parts of your garden and squeeze them into balls. If the ball keeps its shape and feels sticky, it has a high clay component; if it falls apart, it is light and silty or sandy. Aim for soil that is somewhere in between these two, by adding plenty of organic matter (such as manure, garden compost, mushroom compost – which is slightly alkaline – or leaf mould) at a minimum of a bucket per square metre. If you have a heavy clay soil, also mix in plenty of grit or sharp sand to aid drainage. Another important test is to determine how acidic or alkaline your soil is, as this will affect the range of plants you can grow. Simple pH-testing kits are available from most garden supplies shops.

TOPSOIL
Every garden has a layer of topsoil with the subsoil underneath. Aim for a minimum of 30 cm of topsoil in planting areas – although the deeper the topsoil the better, as this is where most of the nutrients are stored. Try to design your garden utilising the best and worst soil areas and so avoid having to move huge amounts of earth. For example, areas of mainly subsoil may be best for the hard landscaping,

keeping the good topsoil spots for the planting areas. Areas where subsoil has been brought to the surface simply cannot be planted, aren't worth trying to condition and will need to be taken off site. A good design will keep this down to a minimum, as it will get expensive. Sometimes this simply can't be avoided and you may decide that it's worth the initial costs to implement your design. The time you spend in getting your soil right will be paid back to you ten times over in the long run.

BRINGING NEW SOIL TO LIFE
If you have brand new topsoil it is likely that it will be sterile. Look to add as much organic matter as possible, by digging in or mulching over the soil to a minimum of 5 cm, and throw in as many earthworms as you can, as they will help do the job for you. I bought a bagful of worms online and, as well as amusing the kids when they came through the letterbox in a breathable bag, they have been the hardest workers in my garden ever since! If you are going to be planting new trees and shrubs also incorporate some mycorrhizal fungi. It helps the plants to develop their root systems, enabling them to absorb more nutrients and moisture.

DEALING WITH COMPACTION
During construction work there will always be some displacement and compaction of topsoil and subsoil. You can help restore the soil here by digging – or rotovating – it over, aiming to get as much air back into the soil as possible, before undertaking any planting. This can be done at the same time as incorporating any extra organic matter or drainage material. It's a messy job and a real pain, but make sure that the soil is tip-top, even if that means waiting a few months because the soil is too wet or frozen and therefore unworkable. Once the soil is planted, it's almost impossible to go back and do it properly without taking all the plants out and starting again.

In a shady sloping garden it's important to separate out the planting from the usable areas. In this garden, building the terraced retaining walls in steel offers up the opportunity to import some new topsoil as well as conditioning the existing soil to create distinct, fertile planting areas. A tree fern and ground cover ferns, as well as the snowy woodrush *Luzula nivea* in the foreground, all grow happily to create a lush feel.

being clever with your space

Good design is all about getting the most from your space. But when you're in it, it shouldn't feel as though you're intentionally trying to be clever, as it will often turn out gimmicky.

MAKE A LIST

The first thing to do is write down a list of everything you want to use the garden for, which will quickly focus the mind and form a kind of brief for what is realistically achievable. If you live with someone else or are part of a whole family then get them involved at this point, too, with everyone throwing in ideas earlier rather than later.

Start with your basic needs, discussing exactly how you plan to use the garden – for entertaining, relaxing, playing, working, a bit of gardening, yoga, sunbathing, etc. Once you have identified the main uses, move on to some more detail, such as what type of entertaining you do and how many people you expect to have round. Is it six to sit and dine alfresco? Or is it more like ten or twelve gathered for relaxed drinks? What games do you or your kids want to play? Basketball? Football? Finally, write down your practical needs, such as a washing line and storage, etc. to complete your list.

DRAW IT OUT

Whether you can draw well or not, try to produce a few different sketches to explore different layouts. As you draw, think about your list and consider particular areas for certain functions. Sunbathing areas will obviously need sun and you may prefer dining areas to be close to the house for ease. A few key decisions such as these will help make sense of the space and help it all fall into place. Of course, it's unlikely that you'll have enough space to define individual areas for each need, so plan with flexibility in mind and look to double up the use of areas where possible. Can a main seating area also be somewhere the kids can play with a smaller

area off it for the barbecue? If you know small walls are going to be built can they double up as informal seating?

Some of your wish-list may simply not be achievable. Although my garden is a family garden, it just wasn't possible to design it so as to be able to play much football in it, so that was sacrificed for other needs; we go and play football in the park round the corner.

DIFFERENT LAYOUTS

Consider turning a conventional garden around completely and positioning the main seating area at the back of the garden. Try to visualise how this would look. If your garden is north-facing and long enough then maybe that's the sunniest area. Could it also be the easiest place to create some extra privacy? It'll also give the garden a destination and a sense of journey.

Long thin gardens need the long-view to be broken up with planting coming in from either side. Look to put the layout at an angle, which in turn will create triangular shaped planting areas, creating movement and interest.

The seating area at the back of the garden transforms the way the space is used. Contrary to a traditional layout, consider creating generous seating areas away from the house. For an integrated look, plan them into the layout during the design stage.

where to eat
This seating area makes good use of a shady spot, is an extremely efficient use of space, and adds focus and direction to the overall design. If you are ever putting in walling to retain soil, consider tying in a custom-made seating area and having a table made up to fit.

create angles
This entire garden has been designed tilted onto an angle, with the lines carried right through the entire space. It breaks up the rectilinear boundaries as well as giving the garden movement and flow. The triangular planting areas cut into it on different levels to break into the main area.

archway
This simple archway crosses the whole garden. It was built from copper pipes and old scaffolding boards set onto timber posts. Although the timber deck provides a raised surface, the structure above eye level subtly helps to delineate the areas as well as punctuating the space above your head.

the illusion of space

triangular shed
Although this isn't the most spacious of sheds, it does work well within the lines of the garden and is only used to store a few tools and cushions. A standard rectangular shed would be difficult to screen and would eat up a lot of valuable space in this small garden.

grapevine
Bringing extra planting in at ground level can be difficult as space can be limited. A pergola provides the perfect opportunity to up your garden's proportion of greenery, in this case with a climbing grapevine. There's plenty of space overhead to take advantage of!

cockle-shell mulch
All the planting areas have a drip irrigation system built into them, and are covered by a landscape fabric and a cockle-shell mulch to considerably reduce maintenance. The shells are lightweight, but they are also light in tone and texture, adding to the garden's spacious feel.

There are many clever ways to make a small garden seem bigger and to create the feeling of a more generous space. Often, when I've cleared out an overgrown garden my clients say that they can't believe how big their garden is. It's important to try and keep this sense of openness, but also to add in elements that will create interest and mood in what would otherwise be the most boring garden on Earth.

HIDE BOUNDARIES
Seeing all the garden boundaries at once means that you will know immediately exactly how big it is. Covering them fully (or at least partially) with planting creates an illusion that the garden may go on further, linking it to the extended landscape.

PLANT AND LEAF SIZES AND COLOURS
In small gardens it's a common mistake to use small, low-growing plants, which won't have any real impact on the space. In fact, a few taller plants, such as palms or small trees, placed generously apart will immediately hold the space around them, like sculptures in a gallery. Large-leafed plants in the foreground and smaller-leafed plants towards the back of the garden will increase the feeling of space, by creating a false perspective. Silver-foliaged plants and cool-coloured flowers will give the impression that it is receding into the distance.

THE LONGEST VIEW
The view from one corner to the corner diagonally opposite is the longest view in a garden. Try to make the best use of it by drawing the eye from one to the other through some clever planting or by placing a simple focal point in between.

GENEROUS AREAS
Any flexible living areas should be kept as generous as possible to stop the garden feeling cramped when it's being used.

It may be worth getting bespoke containers for roof-terrace plants, so that you can dictate their precise heights.

creating privacy

To me, a city garden is somewhere to escape to and be relaxed in. It's impossible to feel completely at ease if we can be viewed from all directions. Of course, urban life is all about living alongside other people, but we want at least one area of our garden where we can be secluded, away from prying eyes, to read a book in, do a spot of private sunbathing or have a few friends over for a drink. It's so easy to create seclusion through plants or structures, even if your garden is overlooked from every single angle, including above. This should be a key factor when designing the layout and deciding where to position any seating areas, as there may be somewhere that naturally lends itself to a private spot.

A single well-placed tree or shrub, a hedge or a mixture of planting that combines enough volume and height will work well. I often use clump-forming bamboos, such as *Phyllostachys* and *Fargesia* to create a vertical 'living screen', which helps to block out specific views onto seating areas from on-looking windows. Evergreen shrubs such as *Photinia*, *Viburnum tinus*, *Laurus nobilis*,

Pittosporum tobira and *Osmanthus frangans* will all do the job, whether planted formally or informally, but also think whether you need evergreen plants. Will you need the cover in the winter? Deciduous shrubs such as *Cotinus*, *Cornus*, *Sambucus nigra* and *Euonymus alatus* are also wonderful screening plants and can easily be pruned to a desired size.

Consider the required height of any planting when you are sitting in the garden, as it may not need to be as high as you think. If you are overlooked from above, think about planting a small tree with a good canopy and a clear stem of at least 2.2m. The hawthorn *Crataegus prunifolia* or crabapple *Malus floribunda* are ideal and they will also add plenty of seasonal interest with flowers, fruit and autumn leaf colour, as well as encouraging wildlife into the garden. If you live in a sheltered part of the world, then the exotic, evergreen loquat, *Eriobotrya japonica* is a good choice.

Structures such as pergolas, gazebos or even free-standing walls can create instant privacy from day one, and, of course, they create the opportunity to grow some fabulous scented

above **Try to keep the focus within a tiny garden. Here the lounger faces away from the overlooking properties and a combination of pots and plants creates the seclusion.**

3 TIPS TO INCREASE PRIVACY

In a garden that is exposed all round you can't completely avoid being overlooked. Create seclusion within it by adding divisions or planting in the key areas where you want to sit, relax or sunbathe.

Consider the view from your eye-level. When you're sitting down, the screen may not need to be so high.

It may be worth investing in a key large specimen plant or two to do the job instantly, rather than waiting for plants to mature or using trellis.

below **Sometimes a view can't be lost entirely, but with clever design and planting the windows can be obscured and the feeling of privacy from inside greatly increased.**

climbers, too. Make sure to incorporate these sorts of structures into the initial design, as they will always be dominant in a small space, and be sure to choose the dimensions and materials carefully. Prefabricated products made from wood may be easy to buy and install, but they can often feel a little 'heavy' in a contemporary town garden. Lighter materials, such as bespoke metalwork or simple tensioned yachting cables, can give plants the support they need without looking too chunky. And if they are made to be strong enough, they can also be used as a frame to drape an awning across to increase privacy and shade.

Cheaper screening products, such as off-the-peg trellis or willow, heather and bamboo screening (which is available in rolls) can all be erected on posts to create an immediate vertical screening structure within a garden. But be very careful about where you position these as they can often feel 'plonked' in as an afterthought.

ugly walls and fences

The smaller your garden is, the more dominance the boundary walls and fences, and any visible exterior house walls, will have over it. It is important, therefore, to make sure that they work with your design, rather than detracting from it or vying with it for attention. This should be part of your initial planning as it may affect your budget as well as having implications on any planting.

Consider whether the walls and fences are made from a complementary material, or one that might spoil the look that you are aiming for. Knocking down, digging out and removing the spoil and then rebuilding a new wall with an attractive finish can quickly eat up your budget, so make sure that this really is a necessary course of action before embarking on any drastic construction work. Dirty old brick walls may just need repointing and a good pressure-wash to get them looking pristine.

Cheap panel fences are a false economy, so if you are going to put up a new fence look to invest in a higher quality one and see it as an opportunity to forge your garden's style.

If the existing boundaries are structurally sound then there are many ways to disguise them and lose them visually. Or you may want to emphasise them and make them into a feature of your design. Consider where the boundaries can be seen from in your new layouts, to avoid spending a lot of time and money on areas that won't be seen much.

If there are areas of soil at the base of your walls and fences then careful planting can be used to soften their appearance. Excavating a few planting holes through any paving will also usually work out cheaper than vast expanses of cladding material. For year-round cover look for evergreen plants that are 'clothed' down to the ground, or which can be trained or pruned to shape. Climbers, such as ivies, *Trachelospermum jasminoides* and passion flowers are good, as are wall shrubs like *Garrya elliptica* 'James Roof', *Itea ilicifolia* or *Teucrium fruticans*. These can all be trained up a wall or along a wire framework, and are good for 'total' coverage. You can also create simple shapes out of wire frames over which to train well-behaved climbers. This helps to formalise the space and will introduce an extra decorative element. They will need to be clipped regularly to keep them in shape.

A cheaper, short-term option, which works well for smaller sections, is to clad parts of wall with exterior ply-board and then paint it or use screening that comes in a roll. *(See Jazzing Up, pages 148–9 and 156)*

You can also clad walls in sheets of metal – such as sheet steel that has been left to go rusty, zinc and stainless steel. This will give your garden an industrial look, but it can work very well in an urban setting, echoing the surrounding buildings and architecture. The cost of this will vary enormously. You will need to make sure that the existing wall is structurally sound and that the sheets are extremely securely attached. You may also need to attach a wooden frame first.

There are a number of companies that specialise in cladding, and they will be able to advise you on the best solution. They will also have a large range of products specific for your needs, so it's well worth exploring all the options first.

I usually find that a combination of cladding and planting gives the best results and can often turn an unsightly boundary into an attractive key feature.

left In my last garden I disguised an ugly wall by fixing a few sheets of exterior ply-board to it and painting it with deep red masonry paint. I sawed the rootball of a fishpole bamboo, *Phyllostachys aurea*, into single stems and kept it well-watered to create a simple and economic, yet effective boundary.

below The rusty orange finish of Corten steel looks great in a modern city garden and can be used to clad unsightly boundaries or built as a free-standing wall. Here, the vertical lengths of timber set in the planting divide the garden up and create dramatic silhouettes against the steel.

above The easiest way to disguise the boundary is to stain the fence a neutral colour, in this case grey, and plant on it and in front of it. The combination of the well-behaved, evergreen climbing *Trachelospermum jasminoides*, perennial *Verbena bonariensis* and the low-growing *Pittosporum tobira* 'Nanum' at its base adds plenty to the garden as a whole.

mirrors: double take

In small gardens, as in houses and apartments, mirrors can work extremely well to create a sense of space. Even though, of course, the space is purely an illusion, it's this 'feeling' of space rather than the space itself which can make or break a garden.

Real mirrors are a 'no-no' for the garden, as, being made from glass, they are a major safety hazard. They are also extremely hard to seal around the edges, so water will quickly creep in and the backing will start to peel away from the mirror. The professionals use mirrored Perspex or mirrored stainless steel. Both are readily available with pre-drilled holes to make them easier to secure in place with mirrored screws. A poorly placed mirror will look dreadful in a garden setting, so before ordering and installing one try to work out precisely where it should be placed and how big it should be. A common error is to install one that is far too small, which ends up looking horribly twee, or one that is placed in a too obvious position.

The first consideration should be: 'What are you going to see reflected in it?' If the answer is yourself or the back of your house, then this will immediately shatter the illusion and you're far better off without one.

Sculpture, large pots or focal specimen plants such as palms are usually too obvious, as you're simply looking to turn one object into two. Non-descript planting comprising of loose, naturalistic flowers and foliage will be much more successful and the overall effect far more subtle.

Mirrors provide a great way of bouncing light into and around the garden. An ever-changing composition of sky with clouds rolling past makes great subject matter for mirrors and keeps the garden alive with its movement and continual changes in natural light.

A mirror shouldn't be the first thing you see when you enter the garden; a side-wall is usually the best choice for positioning mirrors. They can also be fixed at an angle in order to achieve a specific reflection.

In my view, the larger the mirror the better. I think they look more impressive and the illusion is far more successful if they cover a large expanse of wall. A large mirror fixed directly onto the entire face of a brick pier or free-standing wall can be extremely effective and often playful, too, as its edges cut cleanly across any surrounding planting.

N.B I do have to point out here that many bird-lovers are, quite rightly, extremely concerned about the use of mirrors in gardens. Birds can get duped by the reflections and fly into the mirrors at full speed, often badly hurting themselves and sometimes it can even result in their death. Make sure to place them only where they won't be seen by birds flying at speed, such as side walls, in side alleys or in extremely small gardens or basement areas.

If you choose to install mirrors, make sure that they are large enough to make plenty of impact. Here, the mirrored wall is placed behind tall perennial planting, grasses and old-fashioned roses. The tall, wispy grass, *Stipa gigantea*, is ideal, as it creates a semi-opaque screen at eye-level, increasing the depth of field overall.

in the shade

Tall apartment blocks and houses in the city, combined with overhanging neighbouring trees and imposing protective boundaries, result in many urban gardens being extremely shady for large parts of the day, with some receiving no direct sunlight at all. Although we usually can't control the amount of light our gardens get, we can make the most of any that is available and plan accordingly. Shade is often seen as a hindrance when it comes to planting, but there are actually more than enough great plants that grow very happily and work beautifully in the shade to give a city garden a cool lush feel.

LOSE THE LAWN
If you have been persistently struggling with your shady lawn areas and are still left with a muddy patch, it's because lawn, which is made up of a mixture of grass varieties, simply doesn't thrive in shade. So far I haven't found that any of those 'shady special' lawn mixes do the job either. Consider it as an opportunity to lighten your workload and completely change the gloomy feel by putting down a material that actually works in shade.

LIGHTEN UP
When introducing new materials to your garden, such as paving, walling or furniture – or even when painting existing elements – see it as an opportunity to really change the mood of the space. Avoid dark materials like slate or black basalt, and instead look to use lighter-toned materials, such as natural sandstones, white granite and pebbles. Light materials will bounce any available light around the garden, really helping to lift shady areas. And you will find that your plants actually respond to the increased light levels, too.

To get an idea of the existing tones in your garden, look at it through half-closed eyes. You will see it in shades of black and white, rather than colour, so you'll be able to identify the darker and lighter areas.

A single imposing element such as a bleak tall brick wall brings down a garden, even when the rest of it is working well, so look to transform areas like this and make them work with the rest of the garden. Avoid building dense structures such as pergolas, or dividing the garden up with tall hedges or trellis as it will only make it feel gloomier, and go for a more open-plan layout.

SHADY PLANTS
Although there are many plants that thrive in shade, you will probably have to aim for more of a foliage composition than a riot of colours, and introduce shots of colours through bulbs and some annuals. Forget about trying to grow sun lovers like lavenders, achilleas and pinks, as they will only under-perform, not flower properly and grow leggy, and you will be left feeling frustrated. Instead, look for shade-loving plants that thrive in these conditions, as they will always look in peak health.

Plants that have glossy leaves, such as bergenias, camellias, skimmias, sarcococcas, daphnes, hellebores and asarums are all fabulous in the shade, as they have specifically adapted to make the most of any light that is available and to help bounce it around as much as possible.

Variegated plants such as *Pittosporum tobira* 'Variegatum', variegated hostas (if you can keep 'em slug and snail free!), variegated ivies and hollies are especially useful, too, as they will help to lift dark areas purely through the light pigmentation in their foliage.

Ferns and Japanese maples are also shade lovers and will help to add depth to the textures of a shady retreat. Although silvery leaved plants are usually associated with plenty of sun, the silver-leaved and architectural *Astelia chathamica* 'Silver spear' and the smaller, more coppery *Astelia nervosa* 'Westland' both do well in shade and help to lift a composition with their interesting shapes and colours.

In a shady garden, it's important to grow plants which will thrive. This courtyard lets natural light into the lower ground floor, and is also viewed from above at balcony level. The bamboos, bananas and ivy love the protected microclimate, green up the area and look good from both levels.

sun spots

If you have a south-facing garden, without any surrounding buildings or trees casting shadows over it, then it could be that it receives too much sun. My garden is south facing and gets plenty of rays, but, personally, I can't stand sitting in the heat during the summer months and will always search out cool shade. I don't want my children sitting or playing in full sun either for obvious health reasons.

CREATING SHADE

There are simple ways to create temporary and permanent shade to work with the style of your garden. Just as tall planting can increase privacy levels, it can also create shade. Trees with spreading canopies will cast a wonderful dappled shade that is perfect for sitting under.

Fixed structures such as pergolas and gazebos will also do the trick, but be careful to make sure that they are in exactly the right place and at the right height to actually give you the cover you need during the summer months (remember that the sun will get higher in the sky, and the position of the shade will move). Also consider how the garden will look with a permanent structure during the grey winter months – they can sometimes make areas of the garden dark and dank, and, if fixed onto the back of a south-facing house wall, can also make the interior gloomy during the winter months when you need as much light inside as possible.

Temporary sail shades, awnings and parasols are available in a wide range of styles, many of which fold up very small so that you can store them easily. They give you the flexibility to move them around with the sun. When you install them, make sure that you use extremely strong fixings (look in yachting chandlers), as they can catch the wind. Make sure to take down in the evening and during windy periods.

MATERIALS

In a hot sunny garden, light, almost-white materials will only increase the feeling of heat and glare, and, unless you are a sun worshipper, you may find it a bit overwhelming; think about using darker tones instead. Decking sits comfortably in hot gardens when softened with looser perennial planting and grasses. Some people worry about splinters when walking in bare feet on the wood, but a high-quality deck should be smooth enough. A lush lawn can work well visually and will certainly help to cool the garden, but during the hot summer months it will need plenty of watering to keep it green.

PLANTING FOR SUN

Many styles of planting thrive in hot, sunny gardens, although their suitability may depend on your soil type. Be careful not to mix too many different styles together, as the garden will become confused. Exotics, such as palms, cordylines, bananas and bamboos will create shade with a lush tropical feel and the plants will help to cool the air through transpiration. A more Mediterranean planting style, with silver lavenders, stachys, artemesia, eryngiums and rosemary etc., will work if the soil is well drained. Succulent plants, such as echeverias, sedums and crassulas are great in extremely hot, dry areas, as they are drought tolerant and extremely low maintenance. They also work well in containers. Mulch over the roots with gravel to help keep whatever moisture there is in the ground and to stop the roots 'cooking'.

WATER

The sight and sound of water can really help to create a cool and refreshing atmosphere, and moving water stirs and cools the air.
(See Stress Busting, pages 118 – 121)

I'm a big fan of sail shades because they help to style the garden and can be put up in no time. Remember that they do need taking down when not in use, as they are designed to catch the wind!

This garden had a new boundary wall built, and so a new garden gate and bin store was constructed at the same time for easy access and integration into the design as a whole. A couple of bamboos help to screen it from the house.

storage

Before you decide on what type of storage to invest in, you first need to identify exactly what you are going to store. I have seen so many sheds and storage spaces full to the brim with absolute rubbish, so that you can't even get into them to get anything out! The most important rule of storage is to be extremely organised. Only keep the essentials and avoid using the space for the overspill from your interior belongings.

SHEDS

Conventional sheds are often the best value for money, even if you plan to take the basic construction and customise it. Plan where it's to go and then disguise it with planting, painting or cladding and add a green roof to replace the green space lost beneath. Make sure there is easy access to the main door and think about how things will be stored inside.

BUILT-IN STORAGE

Building storage into the garden can be a clever way to make use of any 'dead space'. Think about making the most of areas that would otherwise be unused, such as under exterior stairs or fire escapes or to the side of bay windows. These are often awkward places to get any value from. Timber is by far the easiest material to use, but make sure to use treated wood and exterior-grade ply. If you want to make your storage completely watertight, then the materials you use and its construction need to be carefully considered, and should be along the same lines as the construction of a shed. Think about the fall of water on the roof and where that water will go, and whether any of it can be saved in a water butt. Be sure to raise the floor off the soil or concrete to keep it dry, using bearers or the new modular base system.
(See Suppliers, pages 170–1)

UNDER-SEAT STORAGE

If you are going to have built-in timber furniture, consider constructing the seats with lids, to make use of the space underneath. Making the seating attractive and completely watertight is not an easy endeavour, but try to build it so that the excess water runs off to

above Green roofs are a fabulous way of replacing lost foliage in a garden when ground space has been given up to sheds, garden offices or bin stores. Sedum matting is available in rolls and is the lightest and easiest to install, and will encourage plenty of wildlife into the city garden.

above Bicycles are always difficult to visually lose in a small garden, but this is a really clever solution. By building storage in amongst other planters and growing ivy on the roof, it pretty much disappears altogether.

give it the longest possible lifespan. I tend to build storage with the intention of buying watertight storage boxes to put inside. There are also some pretty good pre-fabricated bench units with built-in storage available.

BICYCLE STORES

You can buy pre-built bicycle stores, which can be fitted into either a front or back garden and locked up for security. None of them are particularly attractive and they do eat up the space, so if you need to store more than one bike, consider using wall brackets, combined with a good bike cover and position it in a side-alley or along a strong boundary wall.

BIN STORES

Bins can be extremely unsightly but you do need to ensure easy access for the collectors. They tend to disappear more easily when they are custom-built and designed to relate to the details around them, such as a gate, fencing or trellising. Painting them black often helps to make them less obvious, too.

POINTS TO CONSIDER

● Successfully integrate your storage into the rest of the garden by using the same materials as in the existing design, rather than introducing new ones
● If you go for an off-the-peg shed or storage unit, customise it by cladding or painting it to complement the colours of your garden
● Using darker colours will help units to recede into the distance
● Create storage all in one place; it will look neater and make for easier access
● Whenever you are building new timber structures, such as decking or seating, consider integrating extra storage into it
● Remember to make sure that water is able to freely drain from the base or build in a false bottom
● Always use rustproof fixings and make sure all materials are weatherproof
● Consider creating a false end to a section of your garden to completely hide any larger storage units

dealing with levels

Steps and level changes in a garden don't have to be so obvious that they look like an outside staircase. Here, stone slabs have been set at even heights into a bank, to deal with the level change and then planted in and around for a far and more interesting look.

Gently sloping gardens are often seen as being rather daunting to deal with. Personally, I relish the challenge, and find it often leads to a more interesting final design than a scheme that has been laid out on a perfectly flat level. Interesting planting areas often evolve as a result of the different levels, meaning that plants get viewed at a variety of heights. Extreme level changes are, however, a different story. They will devour your budget, as well as eat into the usable space due to the need for steps and balustrades.

WHERE TO CHANGE LEVELS

It's cheap and easy to draw a line on a piece of paper to mark where a wall is to go, whereas major earth moving and rebuilding is both hard work and expensive! Moving a retaining wall even half a metre one way or the other can make or break your budget, so carefully consider all the implications before you decide to rearrange the walls.

STEPS

In my view a good set of well-designed steps makes a great garden feature, tying in the architecture of the garden by providing some physical direction. Wherever possible, make your steps as generous and approachable as you can, so that they invite you to walk up and down them, rather than mean little things which you need to line yourself up with before attacking! The risers need to be even and a maximum of 20cm (8") and the treads should be a minimum of 30cm (12").

DRAINAGE

Of course, water will only flow one way and new level changes will significantly affect this. Make sure to fill behind walls with shingle and put in 'weep holes' at the bottom, so that water doesn't build up behind. Steps need to have a fall built into them to stop puddling, which could make them dangerous.

TERRACING AND WALLING

Most walls over 60cm (2ft) tall will need expert installation, especially if they are retaining soil; it's just not worth trying to do yourself. If you are cutting steps into a slope or bank, then remember that side walls will be needed to retain the soil. If the level change is great and you are looking at large expanses of side wall, consider stepping these walls to form terracing. The different levels can then be surfaced or planted up to make the best use of the space. This will also help soften the walls.

BALUSTRADES

By law, any level change over 60cm (24") needs a 1.2m-high balustrade. Think carefully about this and any key views that may be affected as a consequence. Terracing these areas in levels of 60cm and under or extending the steps widthways may offer a better solution, avoiding the need entirely, or at least reducing the quantity of balustrade required.

MATERIALS

Deck is a fabulous material for floating over slopes, as it's free draining and doesn't require major foundation work. Steel frames with steel grid surfaces can be made up, complete with steps, to deal with bigger level changes. They can also be used to create, say, a new balcony/breakfast area at first-floor level, incorporating some steps down into the garden to add strength. Timber railway sleepers are probably the most cost-effective way of building low walls and steps and make a good DIY project. Build a framework of sleepers and then backfill them with plenty of loose, free-draining material to form the treads, such as beach pebbles, or plant in and around the steps and walls to help soften them. Building solid walls and steps out of stone or brick, or rendered walling — or a combination of the two — will add a sense of permanence, but will require foundation work.

inside out

Many of us are looking to blur the distinction between the interior and exterior of our homes. This helps to bring the outside in and, in turn, the inside out. Houses are now being refurbished with this in mind and the process opens up the opportunity to consider the design of the two spaces at the same time, and how you might maximise their potential use.

CHANNEL GRATES AND DAMP-PROOF COURSES

Moving from inside to outside while remaining on exactly the same level is safer and easier. It also helps, psychologically, with the flow between the two areas. Depending on the design of the doors and the threshold, channel grating can be laid along the wall to create a consistent level. Slot drains (where the drainage channel is visually lost in a 1cm joint between the paving, so that the paving can be brought level with the interior and right up to the house wall) are increasingly popular. If the doors are already set, it's important not to breach the damp-proof course. You can, however, sometimes retrofit a deck close to the house wall and then fill with large, free draining cobbles to create the effect of the same level. Be careful with precise levels of damp-proof courses and seek professional advice before any installation.

This garden has pared down the garden elements to the very basics to create an insular, minimal space, which is a pure extension of the interior. The surfaces are level throughout, the worktop inside has been echoed with the same style outside and the glass doors fold right back to provide maximum access.

both inside and outside, as materials will weather differently in the two environments. The outside materials will also need to have a non-slip finish. You can use a natural stone, such as limestone or sandstone, throughout, but the exterior stone will need to be laid with a sandblasted, flame textured or riven finish. Timber interior floors sometimes cry out for a timber deck outside. Look for the direction that it is laid in and the width of each board to help forge the relationship between the two. And remember: exterior deck needs a gap between the boards for drainage. If you opt for a completely different material to use outside, look for complementary colours, tones and unit sizes to make a connection.

PLANTING

Wherever possible I look to bring partially see-through planting, such as wispy tall perennials and grasses, close to the house, so that the connection with the garden is instant. The areas against the walls, on each side of doors and French windows, are often dead spaces anyway. This type of planting also makes the view back to the house from the garden far more interesting, too, especially if the house is of little architectural interest.

LIGHTING

Clever lighting techniques can help to link the areas together throughout the year.
(See Stress Busting, pages 130–3)

KEY VIEWS AND WINDOWS

Look for key views onto the garden from all the windows and glass doors and consider how you might work with them. A window onto planting becomes an ever-changing picture frame.

MATERIALS

The relationship between the interior and exterior materials is important in any garden, but, where there is a strong visual connection between the two — for example, with plenty of glass — it becomes absolutely vital to link the spaces successfully. There are few surfaces with the same finish that can actually be laid

SELECTOR

key structures and plants

The materials that you choose for your garden will dictate its overall style, whilst the plants will breathe the life into it. Successfully combining the two is what will set your garden apart and define its very character. The earlier design sections of this book will have helped you to establish your garden's layout and structure, and how you'd like the different areas to relate to each other. This, in turn, will dictate where any key structures or large plants, such as trees and shrubs, are needed to help it work. Selecting the materials, plants and sizes of plants to purchase is when you start getting into the nitty-gritty of garden design and this will be hugely dependent on your available budget.

Digital cameras and cuttings from magazines are the perfect tools to use as a reference to help you pare down and piece together the right elements for your design. Place the images together in different combinations to help you visualise how the garden will look at various times of the year. Remember my maxim: 'Keep it simple', especially when organising the basic shapes in the garden. Materials should work together with regard to their colour, finish and dimensions. If you want to start getting fancy and more experimental, especially with the planting, then that can come with time, but only once you have established a strong underlying structure to hold the garden together throughout the year.

For most people, selecting plants, with their complicated Latin names, is pretty daunting. It can sometimes feel like a whole new language. Then there is the added confusion of an overwhelming choice on the market at any one time, with many of them being subtle variations on one another. Try not to get too hung up the names, and instead try to look at what the plants do. Where do they thrive? How big do they get? What shape are they? What do their leaves look like? Are they evergreen or deciduous? When do they flower? What colour are the flowers? Are they scented? See the planting as an opportunity to get creative.

Above all, the most important points to remember when deciding on planting are choosing what thrives in your soil and in the site's aspect, and making sure that it will do the job you want it to do. You may have found a plant in a book that sounds like the perfect specimen for a particular spot you have in mind, but it just isn't available anywhere. Some keen plantsmen will wait for precisely the right plant, but in my experience it is better to be flexible, keep deliveries to a minimum and, if you need to, ask the nursery for a suitable substitute.

This balcony uses container plants for a variety of purposes: the multi-stemmed tree creates height and shade, the evergreen hedge increases privacy and acts as a windbreak, whilst the other containers are packed with bulbs for a shot of colour.

what works

underplanting
The choice of the partially shade-tolerant *Hydrangea arborescens* 'Annabelle' planted at low level lightens up what would otherwise be a dark area. Its natural green flowers don't compete with other flower colours.

privacy plants
The backdrop planting of the black bamboo *Phyllostachys nigra* helps to create privacy as well as a foil for the planting in front. Bamboos have a very upright habit, which makes them the perfect choice for small gardens as they don't cast too much shade.

plants for accent
The choice of *Verbena bonariensis* as the main colour accent dotted through the planting at mid-level brings a continuity to the planting as a whole. They are an invaluable, free flowering perennial with strong stems, which means that they use up little ground space and don't need any staking.

hard surfaces
The combination of these hard surfaces forms an interesting textural composition with each of the three materials working alongside its neighbour. Because they are all similar in colour the focus turns to the varying quality of each finish, whether it is gloss or matt, as well as the precise dimensions of each unit.

statement beds
This golden grass *Hakonechloa macra* 'Aureola' has a loose shaggy habit for mass planting and it can tolerate plenty of shade. The introduction of yellow foliage is a brave move in this garden, but it works because it has been introduced confidently, by filling an entire planting area to make a strong statement.

olive trees
Olives are wonderful evergrey trees for small gardens, as they can be pruned hard back to keep them the required size. Here, they have been planted to break up the garden at eye-level and three of them standing to attention in a row adds a simple rhythm.

fence
The neutral colour of the fence in this garden is critical to its success and completes the look. It harmonises the space and blends in with the surfaces, adding another texture. If it were a natural wood finish it would distract the eye rather than helping to tie the garden together.

surface planting
Because the fence works so well with the overall design it can be left visible in some areas with planting at a low level. The glossy fresh green foliage of the evergreen *Pittosporum tobira* 'Nanum' creates soft mounds and will thrive in sun or shade. Here, it's used to break the line at the base of the boundary.

plants

This well-designed mixed-planting style highlights the intricacies of each plant through its relationship with its close neighbour. The tree, a *Cornus controversa*, gives plenty of height, whilst the soft fennel, zingy *Euphorbia* 'Whistleberry Garnet', violet-purple *Salvia nemorosa* 'Caradonna' and *Anemanthele lessoniana* (Pheasant's tail grass) combine beautifully to soften the space between the paving and rusty boundary.

Good planting is all about placing plants alongside each other so that they grow happily and healthily in your garden's soil type and its aspect. It is also important to make sure that they look great together, work with the overall design of your garden and help fulfil any specific requirements you may ask of them – creating shade or privacy, adding height or visual interest at eye-level, for example.

go for a mix of formal and informal planting. Some deciduous plants such as dogwoods or a snake-bark maple will also bring in a degree of interest and structure during the winter months with their coloured stems and bark.

Many wonderful gardens of different sizes and in all kinds of settings have a very strong set of rules enforced through structural planting. Although this may look rather severe and clearly defines the garden's architecture and layout during the winter, throughout the spring, summer and early autumn 'frothier' plants will soften its rigid outline. Minimalist city gardens can look stunning, relying solely on employing evergreen plants as 'living sculpture' to create an almost static year-round composition with just the subtlest of seasonal changes.

Trees and large shrubs will bring height and volume into a small garden and encourage wildlife, whilst climbers make good use of verticals and help to screen and soften boundaries, which is an important demand in most urban gardens. Annuals and bulbs can be used to extend the season and introduce splashes of colour exactly where you want them, either in the ground or in containers. Many people are now (or rather, again) using their garden to grow a few herbs and edibles, as you simply can't beat fresh produce, and there's no doubt that children quickly learn the benefits of healthy food if they're growing it themselves.

Bear in mind the adult size of larger key plants and consider how they will work together. I find it's better to give them plenty of room to grow into and then 'fill in the spaces' with perennials and grasses, which are easier to divide and move around than the trees or larger shrubs.

Achieving a balance within your planting will make your garden feel at ease in its setting, so make sure that you keep standing back and having a look when laying out new plants or pruning existing ones.

The structure of the planting is extremely important, as it will contribute to the garden's year-round form and also act as a backdrop for the seasonal activity of perennials, bulbs and annuals. A definite structure can be achieved through introducing formal linear planting, such as yew or box hedging. Or you could choose to have a much looser feel with a combination of evergreen shrubs, or maybe

trees

Whatever sized garden you have, try to grow at least one tree in it, even if it's in a large container, as it will instantly add substance and impact. I look for trees that will do a particular job for me. Evergreen trees are often slow-growing initially, but, in time, give cover at just the right height and provide a strong structure, whilst also adding to the proportion of year-round foliage in the garden.

Deciduous trees will lose their leaves during the winter months and you will therefore lose any cover that they provide, but they will let more light into your garden when it's most needed. They are often more graceful, too, offering plenty of interest with their flowers, foliage, berries and bark, and many have a more subtle winter interest and beauty with their skeletal silhouettes and emerging buds.

These multi-stemmed *Amelanchiers* are perfect for small gardens, flowering in early spring and then giving vibrant autumn foliage. The blue backdrop helps to define their sculptural shape.

Acer (Japanese maple)

Japanese maples work beautifully in small city gardens and thrive in partial shade. They can be grown in large containers. *Acer palmatum* varieties 'Sango-kaku' and 'Osakazuki' have large seven-lobed leaves that turn a wonderful, intense red colour in autumn.
Eventual height and spread: up to 8m x 10m

Amelanchier lamarckii (Snowy mespilus)

Great as a single or multi-stemmed tree. White star-shaped flowers in early spring with bronze leaves maturing to dark green and then a fabulous fiery orange and red in autumn.
Eventual height and spread: up to 10m x 12m

Arbutus andrachne (Grecian strawberry tree)

This strawberry tree has glossy evergreen foliage and a wonderful cinnamon-coloured trunk. Its white flowers are like dainty white bells and the fruit is similar to strawberries. Although they are edible, they don't taste great! This is a perfect specimen tree.
Eventual height and spread: up to 6m x 6m

Betula pendula (Silver birch)

Silver birch work beautifully in city gardens and the white, peeling bark alone can hold a garden together through the winter months. *Betula utilis* var. *jacquemontii* 'Grayswood Ghost' has great autumn colour when the mid-green leaves turn a clear yellow, and it has yellow catkins in the spring.
Eventual height and spread: up to 18m x 10m

Cercis siliquastrum (Judas tree)

In spring, clusters of pink pea-shaped blooms burst from the new young shoots to cover the tree in colour before the leaves come out. From late summer onwards, large bunches of rich purple pods deck the branches and last well into winter, while the pretty foliage turns light yellow and mahogany in autumn.
Eventual height and spread: up to 10m x 10m

Magnolia

There is a wide range of wonderful magnolias that can be grown as bushes or standard trees. The evergreen *Magnolia grandiflora* will add formality to your garden with its highly scented huge creamy-white flowers that appear in August, but they can take several years to bloom.
Eventual height: up to 18m x 15m

Malus (Crab apple)

These are great for wildlife and seasonal interest. *Malus floribunda* has a profusion of pink buds opening to white or pale blush in mid-late spring, followed by small, golden-yellow autumn fruit which often persist into winter, and which the birds love to feed on.
Eventual height and spread: up to 10m x 10m

Olea europea (Olive)

Silver-grey leaves and tiny, creamy-white flowers in summer. This elegant, evergreen tree is hardier than you'd think and makes an excellent specimen plant for a sheltered sunny spot in the ground or a large pot.
Eventual height and spread: up to 10m x 10m

Prunus (Cherry)

Ornamental cherries provide a stunning display in spring. One of my favourites, however, is the winter-flowering *Prunus subhirtella* 'Autumnalis', which has pink buds and white flowers during milder winter periods, when the garden is otherwise fairly dormant.
Eventual height and spread: up to 8m x 8m

Sorbus (Mountain ash, Whitebeam)

I adore most *Sorbus* trees as they reflect every season. *Sorbus vilmorinii* has feathery foliage which turns a dark crimson in autumn. Creamy-white flowers in late spring are followed by clusters of berries in early autumn, which fade from red to pink, then white, as the season progresses.
Eventual height and spread: up to 5m x 5m

shrubs

Shrubs create the important middle tier in planting and add permanent structure. They are essential in most urban gardens, where space is restricted, as they help to build up the vegetation, where trees would grow too large. Most shrubs can be clipped, pruned and manipulated into various shapes and heights to keep them in scale with the rest of your garden, or to provide screening where you need it. Spring-flowering shrubs will go on to provide the perfect green backdrop for perennial planting and often have stunning autumn foliage. Shrubs are usually quite tough and, once established, will need little work, apart from the occasional pruning.

Abelia 'Edward Goucher'
This elegant, semi-evergreen shrub is ideal for a sunny spot in well-drained soil. Lilac-pink, trumpet-shaped flowers on arching branches throughout the summer with bronze-green, glossy leaves maturing to dark green.
Eventual height and spread: 1.5m x 2m

Buxus (Box)
You simply can't beat a clipped evergreen box to add graphic formal structure to a garden. It is fully frost hardy and will grow in both sun and semi-shade. Why not clip it into funky shapes and decorative hedges? It is very slow growing, though, so requires patience.
Eventual height and spread: There are around 70 species, which grow to a range of heights and spreads

Ceratostigma willmottianum (Hardy plumbago)
Deciduous, low-growing shrub with an open rounded habit. Has intense blue flowers from late summer well into autumn, which look great alongside the wine-red autumn foliage. You will need to cut it back hard in the spring. It is fully frost hardy, but does require sun.
Eventual height and spread: 1m x 1.5m

Convolvulus cneorum (Silverbush)
A species of bindweed, this has silky silvery evergreen foliage with funnel-shaped white flowers from late spring to early summer. Grows well in sun on well-drained soil or in a pot alongside other Mediterranean plants.
Eventual height and spread: 60cm x 90cm

Cornus alba (Red-barked dogwood)
Some dogwoods have vibrant winter stems. This one has green leaves with clear white margins and a crimson red stem. It is best grown as a multi-stem, and will sucker, so don't be afraid to cut it back hard in the spring for good stem colour the following winter.
Eventual height and spread: 3m x 3m

Daphne bholua 'Jacqueline Postill' (Daphne)
A fabulous semi-evergreen upright shrub with the most gorgeous deep purple-pink flowers in late winter. The flowers have the sweetest scent, that, alone, will fill a small garden. Is frost hardy, but does require sunlight.
Eventual height and spread: 2-4m x 1.5m

Hebe topiaria (Hebe)
A dense mound-shaped evergreen shrub with a hint of grey in the glossy sage-green leaves. I use it for low-maintenance gardens that need to have plenty of structure, and I plant them quite close to each other to form soft 'pillows'.
Eventual height and spread: 60cm x 90cm

Hydrangea arborescens 'Annabelle' (Hydrangea)
There are some wonderful hydrangeas that are perfect for the city garden. 'Annabelle' has large flowerheads on long stalks between April and July – spectacular white-green balls that can grow up to 25cm across. Plants are normally very hardy but late frosts can damage the buds, so grow them in a sheltered corner or against a warm wall if your garden is particularly cold.
Eventual height and spread: up to 2.5m x 2.5m

This exquisite planting scheme has a restricted colour palette of whites and fresh mid-greens. The shrubby *Viburnum opulus* has a far looser habit than the blocks of white *Iris sibirica* and foxgloves and the rounded shiny mass planted *Asarum europaeum*. The eye is led through to trunks of the silver birches underplanted with ferns.

Nandina domestica (Heavenly bamboo)
Although not a bamboo, this has tall bamboo-like foliage whose growth turns a deep red in the autumn. It has white star-shaped flowers in summer and purple-red berries in autumn.
Eventual height and spread: 2m x 2m

Osmanthus delavayi (Delavay tea olive)
Sweetly scented white flowers in spring with dark grey-green small serrated leaves. Its natural shape is domed, but it can be pruned after flowering if necessary.
Eventual height and spread: 2-6m x 4m

Pittosporum tobira 'Nanum' (Pittosporum)
A well-behaved dome-shaped shrub with evergreen glossy leaves and clusters of exquisitely scented bell-shaped white flowers in early summer. Thrives in sheltered gardens in both sun and shade. I use it to help add structure and as an alternative to box.
Eventual height and spread: 60cm x 60cm

Rosa glauca (Shrub rose)
A natural-looking species with simple open blooms that are light to dark pink with bright yellow stamens. The leaves turn blue-grey as they mature and fade to subtle autumn reds, making an attractive background to the dark red hips. This is also known as *Rosa rubrifolia*.
Eventual height and spread: 2m x 1.5m

Viburnum opulus (Guelder rose)
A vigorous deciduous shrub with lacecap-like white flowers in late spring to early summer, followed by small red berries and foliage that turns a fabulous red in autumn.
Eventual height and spread: 5m x 4m

left Although it takes up little ground space this single wisteria has a huge impact on the building by softening, greening and breathing life into what would otherwise be a sterile environment.

below The climbing evergreen *Clematis armandii* can be used for a wide range of applications in both sun and shade. Here it scrambles over and through a galvanised steel grid to increase privacy on a balcony.

climbers and wall shrubs

City gardens are often dominated by their boundaries, which you may need to soften or disguise. Climbers and wall shrubs can do the trick, but also see them as an opportunity to get more plants into the garden, without eating into the available ground space.

Evergreens, such as ivy or *Garrya elliptica* (Silk-tassel bush), can be used to provide a simple textural backdrop to the whole garden or to any planting that is grown in front of them. The more showier climbers, such as roses and most clematis, will provide strong shots of colour as well as lush foliage creating a striking visual impact.

Climbers range from extremely well-behaved and easily controlled plants to bullies that will get their hands on anything and everything to survive. The good news is that the bullies can be cut back really hard where necessary, but my advice is to exercise patience and, rather than planting something that may cover a wall really quickly, look to invest in climbers that will fill the space available over a longer period of time.

Chaenomeles (Flowering quince, Japonica)
Ornamental quinces work well when trained as a wall shrub on a shady wall. Their bare twigs are smothered in flowers before the glossy, dark green leaves appear. *Chaenomeles speciosa* 'Moerloosii' has cup-shaped, pink-flushed white flowers in early spring, followed by a greenish-yellow fruit. *Chaenomeles* x *superba* 'Crimson and Gold' has deep red flowers and golden-yellow anthers.
Eventual height and spread: 1.5 m x 2.5 m

Clematis
Clematis come in a huge range of colours, flower sizes and flowering times. *Clematis armandii* is evergreen with glossy lobed foliage and scented white flowers in early spring. *Clematis alpina* 'Pamela Jackman' has blue lantern-like flowers also in early spring, whereas the yellow small-flowered *Clematis* 'Bill Mckenzie' flowers later in summer.
Eventual height and spread: 7 m x 3 m

X Fatshedera lizei (Tree ivy)
This is a self-clinging shady climber. It has large, deeply lobed glossy leaves ideal for bouncing light around in deep shade. It is good trained against a pillar or wall.
Eventual height and spread: 2 m x 3 m

Jasminum officinale (Common jasmine)
There's nothing more enchanting than the scent of jasmine on a balmy sunny evening. It's a great fast-growing plant with white tubular flowers and fine foliage, perfect for covering unsightly sheds or a south- or west-facing wall. After flowering, remove old and over-crowded shoots to keep it under control.
Eventual height: 10 metres

Lonicera (Honeysuckle)
Honeysuckles are grown for their colour and scent, and can be left to scramble over fences or structures. But they do get a bit unruly unless kept in check. *Lonicera periclymenum* 'Serotina' bears fragrant, creamy-white flowers, streaked dark-red purple, from mid- to late-summer.
Eventual height and spread: 7 m x 1 m

Muehlenbeckia complexa
A tight-knit climber with thin wiry stems, small, semi-evergreen leaves and tiny star-like scented flowers. I use it as a dark-green textural cover and backdrop. It can be a bit of a bully when it gets going so don't be afraid to cut it back hard as you would a hedge.
Eventual height and spread: 1 m x 1 m

Parthenocissus (Virginia Creeper)
I find the Chinese Virginia creeper *Parthenocissus henryana* to be the best behaved and least vigorous. It will grow on a shady wall and has deeply divided leaves with white and pink veins, which turn an intense red giving an awesome autumn display.
Eventual height and spread: can be over 12 m!

Rosa (Rose)
Climbing roses may be seen as traditional plants, but they can look stunning in contemporary gardens, too. There are literally hundreds to choose from, but go for one with a good scent, such as the salmon-pink *Rosa* 'Albertine' or, if you've got the space, the deep-purple rambler *Rosa* 'Veilchenblau'.
Eventual height and spread: A wide range of heights and spreads, depending on species

Trachelospermum jasminoides (Star jasmine)
An extremely well-behaved climber clothed to the ground with glossy dark green leaves, which turn a stunning bronze-red in winter. The mid-summer small white flowers are sweetly scented. It prefers a sheltered wall, and I find does equally well in sun or partial shade.
Eventual height: 9 metres

Vitis (Grapevine)
Grapevines are hardy plants and some will fruit if grown outside all year round. Most have a great autumn colour. Look to grow them over a pergola in a sunny spot to create shade underneath. *Vitis* 'Brant' is mainly grown as an ornamental for its rich red and orange autumn colour, whereas *Vitis fragola* 'Bianca' has edible white grapes that taste of strawberries!
Eventual height: There are about 65 species, growing to various heights and spreads

perennials and grasses

Perennial plants produce fleshy herbaceous growth and, although a few are evergreen, most die back right down to the ground each year. The root system will live for many years producing an annual cycle of stems, leaves, flowers and seeds – invaluable to the garden's overall planting, injecting colour and texture from spring right through to the autumn.

Grasses are perennial plants, which will add height, movement and light to a city garden. Although some are shade-tolerant, most are sun-lovers and prefer well-drained soil. The key is to leave cutting them back until the last minute in late winter, so that you don't lose their wonderful form through the winter months. Plant non-invasive clump-forming varieties and if they need dividing then do this in the spring, as they don't like sitting in cold soil through the winter after being split.

Sun-loving perennials

Achillea millefolium 'Paprika'
Masses of orange-red flowers with yellow centres make up the flat plate-like flowerheads, which float above low-growing ferny, aromatic, foliage. There are plenty of other varieties from yellows, through reds to lilacs. They need good drainage and plenty of sun.
Eventual height and spread: 60cm x 60cm

Agapanthus (African blue lily)
Large, strap-like deep green leaves and blue or white trumpet-shaped flowers. 'Black Panther' has dark blue flowers from almost-black buds, whereas the Headbourne hybrids range from sky blues through to whites.
Eventual height and spread: 60cm x 40cm

Echinacea purpurea (Coneflower)
Erect stems with singular daisy-like flowers from mid-summer to late autumn. Has golden-brown cone-shaped discs and purplish-red ray-florets. This is a tough plant, which will add a strong shot of colour.
Eventual height and spread: 1.5m x 45cm

Helenium 'Wyndley'
This robust, upright perennial looks wonderful planted in bold drifts in moist but well-drained spots. It has orange-brown daisy-like flowers up to 8cm across with prominent, brown centres in late summer. It Looks great alongside grasses. Bees and butterflies love it.
Eventual height and spread: 80cm x 50cm

Shade-loving perennials

Anemone hupehensis 'Hadspen Abundance' (Japanese anemone)
Long, upright stems with large open blooms in reddish-pink from mid- to late-summer.
Eventual height and spread: 1.2m x 45cm

Arisaema sikokianum
Weird and wonderful plants that don't look hardy, but they are! In spring, each large, deep purple spathe contains a prominent club-like white spadix.
Eventual height and spread: 50cm x 15cm

Crocosmia 'Jackanapes'
Beautiful, bi-coloured, orange-red and yellow, funnel-shaped flowers on wiry, branching stems in late summer and early autumn, with lance-shaped, mid-green leaves.
Eventual height and spread: 60cm x 8cm

Euphorbia amygdaloides var. robbiae (Wood spurge)
Bushy and softly hairy with reddish-green stems and spoon-shaped glossy evergreen foliage. Flower heads consist of lime-green cup-shaped bracts in spring. Useful as ground cover even in poor, dry soil.
Eventual height and spread: 60cm x 60cm

Most grasses thrive in the well-drained conditions that containers have to offer. They can also cope with strong winds, making them ideal plants for a roof garden. You simply can't go wrong by combining different grasses, as they will always look good and work happily alongside each other.

Grasses

There are simply so many good grasses that will help create a natural look in an urban setting, but here is a selection of my favourites, which I promise won't let you down.

Anemanthele lessoniana (Pheasant's tail grass)
Has a copper tint to the foliage, which will hide the base of taller perennials. It will self-seed around the garden and the seed-heads provide a winter food source for birds.
Eventual height and spread: 1.2m x 1m

Festuca glauca 'Elijah Blue' (Blue fescue)
A dwarf fescue with low hummocks of vivid silver-green evergreen foliage and flowers held above the foliage. Perfect for in-filling and under-planting and ideal for containers.
Eventual height and spread: 10cm x 10cm

Miscanthus sinensis 'Morning light'
A fine-textured grass with cream and green foliage giving it an airy feel. Pink flowers held above the foliage in late summer.
Eventual height and spread: 1.5m x 1.5m

Miscanthus sinensis 'Malepartus'
This fabulous grass can create some real drama. It has feathery, brown-gold flowerheads in late-summer held high above the leaves. The flowers and foliage turn a beautiful red in autumn. It is also wonderful when backlit.
Eventual height: 2m x 1.5m

Stipa gigantea (Giant feather grass)
A real favourite with designers. Forms a low tufty mound of foliage and erupts with tall oat-like flower heads in mid-summer.
Eventual height and spread: 2.5m x 1.2m

annuals and bulbs

Bulbs take up little ground space, but will add so much to a planting scheme. These alliums have finished flowering, but their seedheads still look fabulous floating way above the grasses.

Annuals and bulbs will give you a shot of colour exactly when and where you need it, whether that's under a tree, in-between other plants in your borders or in containers that can be moved around to keep the garden looking fresh and vibrant. Spring bulbs can be planted in the autumn, forgotten about, and are always a joy and a welcome relief when they come up after a long winter. The great thing about annuals, whether raised from seed or bought as plug plants from the garden centre, is that you can have plenty of experimental fun with growing different colours, changing them each year, and hitting on an original combination that works particularly well in your garden.

Annuals

Centaurea cyanus (Cornflower)
Cornflowers look wonderful when their rich blue flowerheads are drifted through perennial planting. They can be sown direct in the autumn and spring for a summer long display.
Eventual height and spread: 90cm x 30cm

Cerinthe major 'Purpurescens' (Honeywort)
An unusual-looking hardy annual with oval, fleshy blue-green leaves, mottled with white, and rich purple-blue, tubular flowers held inside sea-blue bracts. Bees love it. It often self-seeds around the garden.
Eventual height and spread: 60cm x 60cm

Cosmos
Cosmos bipinnatus is a half-hardy annual on stiff stems above fine, fresh mid-green foliage, with a constant supply of vivid pinky-purple or white flowers throughout the summer. Cosmos atrosanguineus (Chocolate cosmos) has velvety reddish-brown chocolate-scented flowers.
Eventual height and spread: 75cm/1.5m x 45cm

Eschscholzia californica (Californian poppy)
A low-maintenance, fast-growing annual with feathery grey foliage and bright orange, red, yellow or white poppy-like flowers. Needs plenty of sun and regular deadheading.
Eventual height and spread: 30cm x 15cm

Helianthus annuus (Sunflower)

Kids love to grow sunflowers and they can look amazing in a city garden. 'Russian Giant' is a monster with a flowerhead up to 25cm across. Or go for the dramatic 'Black magic', which is a dark maroon colour. Sow directly into the ground and mollycoddle for best results!
Eventual height: There are about 80 species of sunflower ranging in height from 60cm to a massive 5m!

Lunaria annua (Honesty)

This biennial has purple flowers in early spring followed by papery, translucent oval seedheads, which dry out and can be left in the garden or taken indoors and used in flower arrangements. Let them self seed.
Eventual height and spread: 90cm x 30cm

Nicotiana (Tobacco plant)

These do best when grown in partial shade. *Nicotiana sylvestris* is the most imposing of the tobacco plants with large lime-green leaves and a mop of tubular white flowers. Some species also have a wonderful scent.
Eventual height and spread: There are around 70 species of tobacco plant ranging in height and spread from 20cm to 3m

Papaver (Poppy)

Simple open flowers are fabulous in early summer. *Papaver commutatum* 'Ladybird' has brilliant red flowers with black markings at the base of the petals — they appear to fly in mid-air! *Papaver somniferum* (Opium poppy) has larger cup-shaped flowers in a wide range of bright colours.
Eventual height and spread: There are around 70 species of poppy (also including perennials and biennials) ranging in height and spread from 15cm to 30cm

Tropaeolum majus (Nasturtium)

A sprawling, trailing, climbing annual with rounded leaves and orange or red flowers. They make good ground-cover or can be grown over the edge of a raised planter. The spicy flowers can be eaten and look great in salads.
Eventual height and spread: 3m x 5m

Bulbs

Allium hollandicum 'Purple Sensation'

One of the best ornamental onions with spherical rich purple flowerheads held on tall stems throughout the summer.
Eventual height and spread: 1m x 10cm

Crocus tommasinianus (Crocus)

Late winter- to early spring-flowering crocus producing one or two slender flowers. Colours vary from silvery-lilac to reddish-purple.
Eventual height and spread: 10cm x 2.5cm

Erythronium 'Pagoda' (Dog's-tooth violet)

A very vigorous species of Dog's-tooth violet with graceful pale yellow blossoms in spring and broad, wavy marbled leaves.
Eventual height and spread: 35cm x 10cm

Galanthus elwesii (Snowdrop)

A robust bulbous perennial snowdrop with broad glaucous leaves. It has honey-scented white flowers from late winter to early spring.
Eventual height and spread: 22cm x 8cm

Iris reticulata 'Gordon' (Iris)

A delicate little iris perfect for a raised planter or rockery. It produces blue flowers with golden-yellow and white throats with a lovely scent in late winter and early spring.
Eventual height and spread: 15cm x 10cm

Muscari armeniacum (Grape hyacinth)

This is the best known of the grape hyacinths. Clusters of small cobalt-blue flowers look like bunches of upside-down grapes.
Eventual height and spread: 20cm x 5cm

Narcissus 'Actaea' (Daffodil)

A very simple, white-flowered daffodil with a yellow centre edged with a 'ribbon' of red. Flowers in late spring with a lovely scent.
Eventual height and spread: 45cm x 8cm

Tulipa 'Ballerina' (Tulip)

Graceful long-stemmed flowers with very striking tangerine-orange pointed petals.
Eventual height and spread: 60cm x 15cm

Many exotic plants have fabulous sculptural foliage and flowers and they will thrive in the protected microclimate that the city has to offer. They look very much at home in urban gardens, as they work extremely well alongside the strong architecture of the surrounding buildings. However, exotics will perform very differently in your back garden than in their native setting, putting on plenty of leaf growth due to the relatively rich soils, but often not quite reaching their flowering period as the length of the summer season or strength of sun is not sufficient. Look for tough plants that will thrive, and appear healthy without the need for constant attention or protection, rather than those that need a lot of care.

Acacia baileyana (Cootamundra wattle)
A half-hardy evergreen small tree or shrub that will survive outdoors in very mild areas. Ferny silver-blue leaves and yellow pom-pom flowers in late winter and early spring.
Eventual height and spread: 7m x 5m

Amaranthus caudatus (Love-lies-bleeding)
This may have been a Victorian favourite, but it looks equally at home in an exotic garden with its long tassels of blood-red flowers in summer and autumn that can reach up to 45cm.
Eventual height and spread: 1.2m x 45cm

Astelia chathamica (Silver spear)
Elegant, sword-like silver foliage with yellow-green flowers in spring. May suffer from frost damage, so will benefit from protection.
Eventual height and spread: 2m x 3m

Beschorneria yuccoides
A succulent with broad, yucca-like grey-green leaves up to 1m long and fabulous red flower spikes in late summer over 2m tall.
Eventual height and spread: 1m x 3m

exotics

Exotics can be used as a living sculpture in the urban garden. The spikes of the rounded *Echinocactus grusonii* in the foreground catch the light and pick up on the yellow flowers and the contrasting form of the *Aloe vera* behind.

Canna x generalis 'Durban' (Indian Shot Plant)
Has a very exotic appearance with purple foliage and bright orange flowers in summer and autumn. It can be left in the ground, but may not flower before the frosts.
Eventual height and spread: 1.2m x 60cm

Cordyline australis 'Cabbage palm'
A good addition to a jungle- or red-themed border. This palm-like tree has long, thin, arching, purple, spear-like leaves. Best grown in a large pot and must be kept in a frost-free spot over winter. When it grows above eye-level you will be able to see its fabulous cork-like trunk.
Eventual height and spread: 5m x 4m

Cyperus papyrus (Papyrus)
An elegant clump-forming moisture-loving rush. It's not hardy enough to leave out all winter but can make a great summer display in a pond or wet tub.
Eventual height and spread: 2m x 1.2cm

Eriobotrya japonica (Loquat)
This large shrub or small, spreading tree is hardy in sheltered places. The dark green, glossy, leathery leaves are attractive all through the year. In warmer locations it has clusters of small, white, fragrant flowers in late autumn and edible orange fruit in spring.
Eventual height and spread: 6m x 6m

Hedychium densifolium 'Assam Orange' (Garland lily, Ginger lily)
Great, lush green foliage and exotic tubular, fragrant orange or yellow flowers in dense cylindrical spikes in late summer. Can be grown as a clump-forming border perennial. Plant in sun or partial shade.
Eventual height and spread: 5m x 2m

Melianthus major (Honey bush)
A truly fabulous architectural plant with blue-grey, boldly toothed foliage. It will spread, so consider trimming back to keep it tidy. From late spring to mid-summer produces brownish crimson flowers on long spikes.
Eventual height and spread: 3m x 3m

Musa basjoo 'Japanese banana'
The hardiest of bananas with huge, fresh green leaves up to 2m long. It can grow in sun or shade but likes protection from wind to stop the leaves shredding. Can develop quite a trunk if protected through the winter. In summer produces pale yellow flowers. May produce fruit, but it will be unpalatable.
Eventual height and spread: 4m x 4m

Tetrapanax papyrifer (Rice-paper plant)
This really is a monster plant, grown for its huge deeply cut, grey-green leaves, which are thickly covered on their undersides with hair.
Eventual height and spread: 5m x 5m

Trachycarpus fortunei 'Chusan palm'
An evergreen palm with classic fan-shaped mid-green fronds up to 1m long and an unusually hairy trunk.
Eventual height and spread: 20m x 2.5m

Bamboos

Bamboos are in the grass family and can be used to create division, hide boundaries and increase privacy in a small garden. They prefer a rich, moist soil, especially during the first few years whilst they establish themselves. Don't be frightened to take out weak canes, prune off lower branches to show off the stem colour, or thin out dense plants to develop a more sculptural shape.

Fargesia murielae 'Jumbo' (Umbrella bamboo)
One of the best clump-forming varieties for a jungly look with relatively small leaves.
Eventual height and spread: 4m x 1.5m

Phyllostachys nigra (Black bamboo)
The slender arching green canes turn a mysterious jet black in their second or third year, off-setting the mid-green leaves.
Eventual height and spread: 5m x 3m

Pleioblastus variegatus
Upright, woody bamboo with hollow, pale green canes. Attractive, variegated white and green foliage.
Eventual height and spread: 75cm x 1.2m

herbs and edibles

Traditionally, the garden has always been a productive place and the revived interest in growing your own produce has extended into the urban garden. The great thing about home-grown food, picked just before eating it, is that you simply can't get it any fresher. You can also control precisely what has gone into it and avoid nasty pesticides and growth hormones. Many of the herbs and edibles that you can grow are also very decorative and will work well alongside ornamentals. Growing fresh food is a wonderful way to get children involved in gardening, too, and will lead to them eating more healthily. Most herbs and vegetables can be grown in limited space, as long as they get enough sunlight, and many look great grouped together in containers.

Herbs

Ocimum basilicum (Basil)
Sweet, aromatic basil with large pale green leaves is grown as an annual. Grow from seed in a pot in full sun if possible, and regularly pinch out the shoot tips to encourage stronger growth and a neater form.
Eventual height and spread: 50cm x 30cm

Allium schoenoprasum (Chives)
This mild onion-flavoured perennial herb can be grown directly in planting areas as its grass-like foliage and rounded mauve-pink flowers in summer make it an attractive garden plant. Also a favourite with bees.
Eventual height and spread: 45cm x 15cm

Anethum graveolens (Dill)
An attractive annual herb with fine, blue-green edible leaves that can be cut and eaten as little as eight weeks after sowing. If left to flower and seed the aniseed flavour is more intense in the seeds. Needs a sunny site.
Eventual height and spread: 60cm x 30cm

Foeniculum vulgare 'Purpureum' (Bronze fennel)
This bronze or purple fennel is a handsome perennial – not to be confused with the Florence fennel grown for its bulbs. Plants develop clumps of feathery foliage and flattened yellow flowerheads.
Eventual height and spread: 1.8m x 60cm

Rosmarinus officinalis (Rosemary)
One of the oldest Mediterranean shrubs in cultivation. It is an essential herb and a great evergreen garden plant which can be pruned into shape, making a good low hedge. It has lovely blue flowers that attract bees and butterflies. Needs to be kept in shape by pruning after flowering.
Eventual height and spread: 1.5m x 1.5m

Salvia officinalis (Common sage)
Shrubby evergreen sage can be grown easily in a pot or combined with other planting in a flower border. It has felty, aromatic leaves that off-set the purple-blue flowers in summer. The purple-leafed variety is even more decorative. Prune into shape in spring if it starts to get leggy.
Eventual height and spread: 75cm x 1m

Artemisia dracunculus (French tarragon)
French tarragon is tastier than Russian tarragon and easier to control. This perennial plant has narrow, pale green, aromatic leaves on rather untidy stems, so maybe grow it somewhere out of sight if possible.
Eventual height and spread: 60cm x 30cm

Thymus vulgaris (Thyme)
Thyme makes a great low-growing, carpeting plant and can be grown in amongst paving, gravel or small shrubby bushes. There are also some golden or silver variegated plants such as 'Doone Valley' or 'Silver Posie'
Eventual height and spread: 10cm x 25cm

A huge range of edibles can be grown in containers in a city garden providing the freshest fruit, vegetables, herbs and salad for the kitchen. Most of them need plenty of sun, so think about where they will be placed in the garden before planting them up.

Edibles

Capsicum annuum (Chilli pepper)
Shrubby plants with star-shaped flowers followed by plenty of fruit. Plant seeds indoors on a sunny windowsill, and then grow outside. The hotter and sunnier the position, the better.
Eventual height: Depends on the variety you choose, but approx 60cm-1m x 60cm

Lactuca sativa (Lettuce)
In a city garden, choose the cut-and-come-again varieties, such as the red-leafed 'Lollo Rosso'. They look good in containers and borders and can be harvested throughout the season.
Eventual height: approx 15cm x 25cm

Lycopersicon esculentum (Tomato)
Sow in late spring under glass, or buy small plants and plant out when the frosts are over. 'Gardener's Delight' is a very popular, reliable variety and 'Tumbler' is a trailing variety, which looks great in hanging baskets. Prefers sheltered sunny positions and even watering.
Eventual height: Depends on the variety you choose, but approx 60cm-2m x 60cm

Phaseolus vulgaris (French bean)
French beans are particularly good for small gardens as the dwarf and bush varieties are both attractive and productive. Dwarf varieties such as 'Andante' are perfect for pots. Climbers such as 'Isabel' or the unusual black pods of 'Cobra' look great growing up a support.
Eventual height: Depends on the variety, but dwarf varieties are usually about 35cm tall

Solanum tuberosum (Potato)
Easy to grow in large containers and delicious when cooked straight from the garden. Go for early, new varieties such as 'Rocket' or 'Swift', or the salad potatoes 'Blue Congo' and 'Charlotte', and grow them in deep pots.
Eventual height: approx 75cm x 75cm

Vaccinium corybosum (Blueberry)
A very attractive shrub and the berry is a superfood. They are partially self fertile, but are more prolific if grown in pairs. Requires acidic soil, so unless you have the right soil, grow in ericaceous compost in a container. Keep moist and place in full sun.
Eventual height: Depends on the variety you choose, but approx 30cm-4m x 1m

Fruit trees
Fruit trees such as apples, pears, plums and cherries look great when they are in flower and will put on good autumn foliage displays, as well as producing plenty of fruit – if you choose the right one. Most trees will need a pollinator planted nearby, and even the self-fertilising ones will generally do better if they are pollinated by another plant. Many can be trained as an espalier onto a warm wall, which will keep the tree productive, contained and make a statement. Obviously be aware of the final size of your tree when considering where to position it.

hard landscaping

The proportion of hard landscaping to soft landscaping tends to increase in the city garden to ensure that it is a practical and usable space. Try to restrict yourself to a maximum of two different materials to make sure that it doesn't become overly fussy in its design.

As you start to make decisions about what will go where in your garden, always consider, in the back of your mind, the practical side of hard landscaping, with regards to what is realistically feasible and which materials are most appropriate. You will find, when you start to investigate landscaping materials (while thinking about budget, finish and unit size) that the choice is actually quite limited – which I

Choose materials based on your budget and their size, colour and tone. It's easy to get carried away trying to combine materials in funky, interesting new ways, but if you focus on the intrinsic beauty of the material it rarely needs to be overly designed to work with a scheme. It's good to get some hard landscaping into a garden, but I find it is most successful when driven by the needs of the garden. Details may be introduced by the necessity to solve a specific problem, such as the transition between two materials, where paving material meets the lawn, the construction of a raised planter, or the configuration of a step formation. Trying to include unnecessary details in a garden can make it look overly ornate and fussy and more often than not actually lead to more problems.

Major structures, such as gazebos, arches and outdoor offices will have a huge bearing on the style of your garden, and the smaller the garden, the greater the need for accuracy when it comes to dimensions. If you can't find exactly what you're looking for as a manufactured product, then go your own way and see it as an opportunity to stamp your own mark on your garden by building something bespoke.

Space in many city gardens is tight and it can become claustrophobic during the actual build. Consider the delivery and storage of materials and plants while work is going on. Can they be left in the street overnight? If so, do you need a permit, and is there a way to prevent them from being stolen? If you are undertaking the project management yourself, or even constructing part of the hard landscaping, plan everything as far ahead as possible. There is a logical order to most landscaping: after any site-clearance and initial levelling work, the boundaries tend to be the first element to go up. Then the garden will be built from the furthest point back towards the house (or other entrance), so that, in effect, you are working your way out of the garden. This helps prevent barrowing and walking on newly laid materials and compacting any soil.

see as a bonus rather than a restriction, as this will accelerate your decision. Locally sourced materials will help a garden sit more comfortably in its extended landscape. Remember, however, that if your chosen material isn't in stock, you may be in for a long wait. This may affect your choice, as may the more pertinent environmental consideration of miles travelled and any possible ethical issues surrounding imported stone.

considerations

The size of each unit you use needs to be carefully planned to work visually with the overall size of the garden. Also consider how it will actually be built: decking and stone both require different sub bases, and precision spacing is vital for a slick look.

Your choice of materials will have a huge impact on the final look of your garden. If your budget is limited, but you're in for the long haul, then it's well worth the up-front investment in high-quality materials with a view to developing the planting when you have more funds. Decide which areas are fundamental to the design, and don't waste your money on any surfaces that won't be used or seen much, such as side alleys or the area around the shed.

USE

Some surface materials are more appropriate for certain positions. Around entrances, solid paving works better than loose materials, as the latter can get dragged around and will quickly become messy. Hard surfaces also tend to work better in seating areas. Loose surfaces will add an element of texture, breaking up solid areas, and combine well with planting.

DIMENSIONS AND DIRECTION

The size of the materials you choose and the direction in which they are laid will help to define your garden's layout and the way your eye moves through it. Keep everything in proportion: smaller units will work well in a small garden. However, large expanses can look fussy and out of scale in larger gardens, so be careful if you are considering something drastic. Large stone flags look great in both large and small gardens, as their 'oversized' dimensions will simplify a small space.

TRANSITIONS

If you do decide to use more than one material, aim for simple transitions between one and the other. Give particular attention to how they will physically work next to each other and how they will be edged. Lawns and gravel areas ideally need a defined edge, for retention of the materials and ease of maintenance. Also consider any level changes and either create a proper step or run everything on the same level. Avoid small 'trip' steps, as these can be very dangerous.

CUTTING

Ideally, look to lay full units with as little cutting as possible. If you do need to make any cuts they should be made within the main area of paving, rather than on the edges, where they are hard to fix and will always look as if they're falling away. Curves look best using appropriate materials such as bricks, which can be fanned out without the need for fiddly cuts. The centre of the circle will get very tight, so will require some precision cutting or consider using a complementary material.

COMPLEMENTARY MATERIALS

I rarely use more than two landscaping materials in a garden, unless the third one is lawn, as it can start to look too busy. How these two materials work alongside each other is very important with regards to their colour, texture and dimensions. It is possible to bleed materials into each other or think about introducing subtle repetitions throughout the garden to help with the movement and flow between spaces. How materials work with the style and finish of the house is also a key consideration. A rendered house wall can always be painted to work with garden materials, but a yellow- or red-brick house will need complementary materials, such as a stone with a hint of yellow. As a rule, the more elaborate the architecture of the house, the simpler the materials in the garden should be.

materials

Visit builders' merchants, stone merchants and timber yards and have a good nose around their stock to get some ideas. Ask for samples to take home so that you can visualise how they'll work with your new design or any existing elements. Don't try to be overly clever with materials and, unless you have a large budget, stick to standard sizes, which will also use standard construction techniques.

DECKING

Decking is a warm, quiet, free-draining material that is extremely versatile. It is ideal for creating simple level changes in a garden or for surfacing a roof terrace. A timber sub-frame, made from treated softwood, is constructed using timbers at least 100 mm x 50 mm, no more than 450 mm apart. They are concreted into the ground on posts with a minimum of 600mm in the ground. On a roof terrace, decking is floated over the existing surface and levelled on bearers without penetrating the actual roof. The top boards can be made either from a hardwood from a sustainable source, such as iroko or cedar, or from a treated softwood. I lay them smooth side up, as the grooves only seem to fill up with debris and get slippy over time.

PAVING

There is a huge variety of paving materials. Make sure you check that they are suitable for exterior use before you part with your cash, as some limestones and travertines may look great but take on moisture and are susceptible to frost damage. Some of the imitations are extremely convincing, durable and good value for money, but they don't have the natural depth of colour, especially when wet. Most of the natural stones will come in a variety of sizes and finishes, from a coarse riven surface, through to a precision sawn finish on all sides, which will give you a slick look. They tend to get more expensive the more they have been passed through the saw. There are some

pre-cut, pre-formed stone circles available in both natural and imitation stone, which are far easier to use than cutting from scratch. Most of these paving materials will be laid onto a 25-50 mm mortar bed over a 100 mm sub base, so the excavated level before construction will need to be approx 150mm below finished level.

TILES

Terracotta or ceramic tiles can be used in gardens, as long as they are frostproof, non slippery and thick enough not to crack if something is dropped on them – a minimum of 10 mm thick. They will need a solid, level, screeded concrete base underneath, and are fixed with exterior, waterproof, flexible adhesive.

GRANITE, SANDSTONE SETTS, DRIVEWAY BLOCKS AND COBBLES

These smaller units are very versatile. They can be laid onto a sand and cement bed, or sometimes straight onto compacted sand over a sub base. Because of their dimensions, they work well in courtyard-style gardens and are very effective if you're looking to form a detailed edge for paving. They can also be used to create a 'soft' path by seeding grass or thyme in-between the joints. And they will work well in driveways, as they can take the weight of vehicles.

BRICK, PAVIORS AND STABLE BRICKS

Both new and reclaimed bricks are widely available. Some can be used as a paving surface, but check before spending any money that they are frost proof. Paviors have similar dimensions to bricks and have been designed specifically for paving and driveways, but be careful of using them in large quantities as they might make your garden look like a car park! Think about the particular bond, such as herringbone, stretcher or basket weave, with regards to the effect it will have on the space and any cutting that may be involved.

Rendered block walls are becoming an increasingly popular choice, as they are more economical than brick walls and also add a contemporary feel to the garden. The smooth surface can be painted to introduce permanent colour to set off any planting, and then repainted to keep the garden looking fresh.

CONCRETE

Concrete is increasingly used as a final finish in gardens. It needs professional installation, as it requires a structural substructure such as a steel reinforcement framework, expansion joints and the correct mix for the application. It can have a colour worked through it prior to pouring or, once it has set, it can be ground with a machine to a variety of finishes.

AGGREGATES

Aggregates can either be laid loose or 'bedded' into a binding material, such as tarmac or concrete. For planting areas and informal paths they can be laid over a landscape fabric at a minimum depth of 50 mm. For paths and terrace areas you will first need to lay a sub base and then the binding layer with the finish on the top. Look to use natural colours and avoid bright colours and white as they'll look brash and date quickly.

METAL GRIDS

Galvanised steel grids will give a contemporary look to the garden and can be 'floated' over areas (a bit like decking), making them particularly useful if you are trying to let light through to a basement below.

verticals and boundaries

Boundaries, free-standing walls, retaining walls and any additional structures such as arches or pergolas – along with some planting – all build up the vertical plane of the garden to create privacy and interest at eye-level. Ensure that structures that will be walked under are a minimum of 2.1m above ground level and even higher if plants are to dangle down from them.

WOODEN FENCES
There are many off-the-shelf fencing products of varying quality that can be used in the garden. They can be left bare, planted over or customised for a more personalised garden. Close board or feather edge fences are built *in situ* using a post and arris rail frame with each board individually fixed to it.

Panels are pre-fabricated and are of varying quality. Be wary of the really cheap products as they aren't made to last long. There are some more interesting and well-made panel fencing products coming onto the market. These include louvred systems, which may not be the cheapest, but are high quality and easy to install.

Trellis can be used as a fence, or added to the top of a fence to increase its height and create an opportunity to grow climbers. If you are putting up trellis at the same time as the fence, use longer fence posts to cater for it, rather than fitting it retrospectively. All these can be used as boundary solutions and as divisions within a garden.

Natural timbers will go a silvery grey over time and you will need to treat all timbers with a seal to extend their life. You could use a coloured preservative or stain, or paint, although this is more difficult to re-apply.

WALLS
There will usually be some existing walling in your garden, either along a boundary or dividing up areas within the space. If you are looking to link walls together visually, then it is important that they are made of the same brick. Builders' merchants will have a range of sample bricks to help you identify the best match, or you may want to use reclaimed bricks to match them exactly. Reclaimed bricks do tend to be more expensive than new ones, though, and there will be a percentage of waste as they won't all be usable.

Although you can have a go at building low walls (under 60cm), proper foundations will need to be dug and poured, and anything higher should be built by a professional. Retaining walls employ a different construction method to free-standing ones, as they are required to hold back a weight load. They will often need a structural engineer to create the initial specification.

Rendered walls are built from concrete blocks, which are then rendered with cement. The cement can have a colour integrated during the mixing process or be left grey, ready to paint. Sleeper walling is great for creating small walls and for dealing with level changes. Fix the sleepers to concreted-in posts using special timber screws. Natural stone walls can make a wonderful key feature in a city garden, but make sure that they have a high-quality finish.

WIRING OVER WALLS
Existing walls or fences can be utilised to create a backdrop for a planting composition. Some climbers need a framework on which to grow – either trellising or wiring – which opens up the opportunity to create interesting compositions with simple shapes. Well-behaved and easy to trim plants such as ivy and trachelospermum can be kept very neat and shaped according to a wire frame. Plants such as climbing roses and wisteria should have their stems kept horizontal to encourage flowering. Small fruit trees such as apples, pears or figs can also be trained onto an appropriate wall using an espalier or cordon, to great decorative effect.

This traditional shed nestles snugly into the corner of the garden. It has been painted green and planting softens its edges making attractive, accessible storage.

source and it's worth designing them yourself, to ensure that they tie in with your garden.

Garden offices are becoming increasingly popular as more people are working flexible hours, including putting in time from home. With a Wi-Fi internet connection the walk to work can become a stroll through the garden. Garden buildings usually don't need planning permission, and are an economic way of adding an extra room to the property. As well as a workspace, they can double up as a gym, spare bedroom or kids' den. Plenty of companies will design and install systems, complete with electrics and heating, and if the room is to be used in the winter good insulation is important.

Be careful when integrating a building into the garden as they can often feel 'plonked' in. The most successful examples are those that are introduced into the design early on and partly hidden and softened with planting.

PERGOLAS AND WALKWAYS

It's always good to break up the space above eye-level and a good way of doing this is with a walk-through, such as a pergola. They will also define the different areas and will provide a 'door' to any 'rooms' that have been created through subdivision of the garden. Although basic kit-form structures can be adapted, I find the best solutions are usually custom-built on site, so that they fit the space exactly. Timber is the obvious choice, but consider modern durable materials such as tensioned cables, steel and polycarbonates. Be generous with any walk-throughs, even if it means stretching them down the entire length of the garden, as it feels unnatural and uncomfortable squeezing through a mean little gap. Over-head horizontals also provide an opportunity to grow a climber or two, so plan a planting space or pocket in any adjacent hard surfaces, so that the climber has a permanent place, and remember that upright post supports will need concrete around their bases to support them.

GARDEN BUILDINGS AND STRUCTURES

Summer houses add plenty to a garden both practically and visually. From a practical point of view they provide privacy, shade, cover and extra storage space. Visually, they instantly add height, give the garden direction and create a focal point, drawing the eye towards them.

There's a huge range of off-the-peg summer houses, from flat-pack designs, to ornate hand-built affairs with fancy finials, which simply demand to be looked at. Contemporary summer houses and gazebos are, however, far harder to

STRESS BUSTING

an outside room

There's no doubt that a well-designed city garden makes the perfect antidote to modern urban living. It can be anything you want it to be: a place to read, to play, entertain, eat, drink, exercise and, of course, garden. Designing your own outside space also provides an opportunity to create a completely individual and personalised exterior 'room' to complete your home. If you are a social being it can be the ideal place to interact with friends, family and neighbours, and if you have children then they can use the garden to release their pent-up energy, play safely and learn about their natural environment.

Too many city gardens are seriously underused and hardly any reach their full potential. A garden's success is heavily dependent on the initial planning and design, which should, from the very outset, consider how the garden is going to be utilised. If the design is carefully considered and executed, then you'll want to be out in it at every given opportunity and will be looking for ways to get the maximum use from it.

The concept of the 'outdoor room' is nothing new and in the city, with space at a premium, it makes perfect sense to see the garden as a room of its own. In my view, the garden must be a room like no other in your house. It should have a very definite mood, so that every time you step into it you are placed in a different frame of mind. It may well relate and link to the interior of your property, but it should be full of life, bringing you closer to, and making you aware of, the nature that your garden – and the surrounding city – has to offer. City dwellers are often so far removed from nature that they forget how fascinating the natural world can be, but I find that reconnecting with it can be one of the most stimulating and therapeutic of experiences. Gardening itself immediately takes my mind off any worries, and it is also a fabulous form of exercise.

Historically, durability was the main factor when designing garden products, especially furniture. More often than not, this meant hard uncomfortable seating – fine in a park, but not something you would want to sit on for long. Fortunately, in recent years there have been plenty of improvements in terms of comfort. Combining modern durable materials with good design has resulted in many fine examples of contemporary garden products being widely available. In turn, this has had a significant impact on the way gardens are used and should be a key factor when it comes to styling them. So, whether you are looking to create a large built-in dining area complete with an outdoor oven or just a quiet place to while away the warm summer evenings, there is something suitable available.

This shady spot is ideal for sitting or lying down
on a hot summer day. Moving water cools the
surrounding air, and helps the mind to escape
the busy city with its gentle sound.

relaxation

I take my relaxation pretty seriously and I find that, after a hard day's work and on the weekends, my city garden is the perfect place to chill out and de-stress from the pace of urban life.

There are several factors to bear in mind to help you to achieve a calming sanctuary. Firstly, it's difficult to fully unwind in an environment that you don't feel completely comfortable in. So, if you are an extremely tidy person then you must have a tidy garden; if you like things a little more loose and wild, then that's how it should be. But remember that there are no set rules − just whatever works for you. Secondly, it's only possible to fully switch off when you don't feel that there's lots of work to be done; if, every time you sit in your garden, you feel guilty for not mowing the lawn, then there's something wrong. Either get rid of the lawn altogether or mow it first, so that you can sit back and relax properly!

Visually, your garden should be a feast of textures and colours, which doesn't necessarily mean an overly vibrant and full-on design incorporating every colour under the sun. A restrained, purely verdant garden can be the most relaxing scheme of all, as you become enveloped within the restful colour, rather than having too many combinations vying for your attention. The beauty of plants is often far better appreciated in more subtle combinations or in the complex variations of a single plant. It is fascinating to look at plants in close detail, whether they are in bud, in leaf, in flower or even fading and decaying

after flowering. Kids love to look closely, too, and a strong magnifying glass makes a great birthday present.

Urban life usually comes with a lively soundtrack, whether it's the background noise of the rumbling of cars or your neighbour's music spilling out of their window. I'd say that that is all part and parcel of living in a metropolis, but if it becomes overwhelming, it is possible to create some sound in your own garden − such as a breeze blowing through some bamboos or the trickle of a water feature to help keep the ear focussed at a shorter range, making you less aware of outside noise.

Also consider scent. It can be intoxicating and is surprisingly seductive. It's easy to find in the form of a flower's perfume or in a plant's aromatic foliage, and can be effectively contained and maximised within the boundaries of a small space.
(See pages 122 − 5)

There are some wonderful city gardens that have been designed with a sense of theatre and pure escapism in mind. You might, for example, choose to take full advantage of the protected microclimate and pack your garden with wonderful exotics to remind you of a holiday destination, or to evoke a particular location, so that every time you step into it you are transported to a foreign clime.

below **Embracing a more minimalist approach helps the city gardener to break away from the traditional and often fussy garden. Simple spaces are ideal for stress busting.**

left **Gardens are rarely comfortable enough, but this cushioned sofa makes an extremely inviting spot. The pergola creates both shade and privacy and painting it white stops it feeling too heavy.**

water features and rills

Moving water can add a whole extra dimension to your garden, bringing both a mystery and a sense of play that static features and installations simply can't compete with. In the heat of summer, water will provide a cool and serene presence, and even the smallest quantity will instantly attract masses of wildlife.

Water is often associated with natural-looking gardens, and is incorporated into a design to give the impression that it has occurred naturally. In an urban garden the notion that any body of water 'happens' to be a part of the natural landscape is simply too far-fetched. Once we have taken this on board we can incorporate the water deliberately and boldly into the garden layout.

It can be introduced in many forms – from a simple pre-fabricated wall-mounted kit or bubble-jet feature, which can usually be customised, to an ambitious succession of waterfalls, fountains or rills. Remember, though, to ensure that the style and particular finish of the feature sits comfortably with the rest of the garden.

Where you position your chosen feature needs careful consideration with regards to what it will 'add' to the garden. Is it to be 'discovered' as you turn a corner, or do you want to be able to hear it first? Perhaps the head of the water feature is at eye-level, a focal point drawing the eye through the long view of the garden?

Getting the size of the water feature in proportion to the garden is also very important. Far too often, invitingly priced, off-the-peg fountains and features are too small for the space for which they are intended, so be careful not to be tempted by something that may look good in the garden centre but will not work in your size or style of garden.

The sound of moving water can create a relaxing mood in your garden, and can be used to detract from the noise of any traffic or close neighbours. If the sound isn't relaxing, however, it can have the opposite effect and after a while it might begin to seem more like a form of water torture! Consider the type and volume of the sound with regards to the style and size of your garden. The height of the fall and the amount of water that it will fall into will affect the sound, so play around a bit. Most pumps are easily adjustable, or you could place something just below the surface of the water – or even in the end of the feeder pipe – to alter the flow and impact, and therefore the sound it creates.

As a variation on a theme, rills can work very well in city gardens. The flow of water from one space to another links areas together in an interesting and engaging way, whilst also introducing subtle movement into the garden. Of course, water can be extremely dangerous with young children, but, under supervision, a shallow rill can entertain kids for hours as they watch their boats float downstream.

With all moving water features it's vital to work out what will happen to the water and how the garden will look if the pump is switched off, or when water is lost through evaporation during the summer.

Whatever you decide, if you choose to include water in your garden, it's important that it is maintained properly. Otherwise, it will instantly deteriorate and quickly detract from the look of the garden by looking messy – and probably smelling bad, too. So, think about its maintenance before you install it. Who will look after it and how long will it take? Questions like these will help you to decide on the scale and type of water feature to build.

Clever use of water can help distract the ear away from city noises such as traffic, while keeping the visual interest focussed within the garden space.

When incorporating water into the city garden make sure it's done with confidence. This large pond with 'floating' stepping stones may look rather treacherous, but it adds a new dynamic to the garden.

ponds

Ponds are fabulous for their reflective qualities; I love watching the movement on the surface of my pond when it is raining. You could even think about incorporating a feature, such as a waterfall or fountain to add some more permanent movement. You shouldn't, however, need to install any expensive filtration systems; ponds should be sustainable and good planting will ensure a high quality of water.

If you have a formal city garden then continue with this theme and introduce a strong, geometric pond, such as a square, rectangle or circle – which are also the easiest shapes to execute successfully. Similarly, if your garden's style is more relaxed, choose something natural-looking.

Think about whether you want your pond to be sunken or raised. What will you see in the reflection in both cases? It's always tempting to sit close to water and so the advantage of a raised pond is that you can build the edges at a perfect seating height. There will also be less spoil to deal with from the digging process. Ground-level ponds with beached edges are better for wildlife, however, as frogs, toads and newts will be able to get in and out easily.

SITE, DEPTH AND CONSTRUCTION

A pond is best sited in a little shade, but away from deciduous trees. (Fallen leaves that drop into the water will quickly rot, increasing the nitrogen levels and turning the water green in spring. It'll smell pretty bad, too.)

Ponds should have a minimum depth of 45 cm, often much deeper, depending on what plants and fish you want to introduce.

There have been many advances made in durable and flexible pond materials with a range of construction methods now available, from concrete ponds with a waterproof render to pond liners that can be bought on a roll, 'box welded' and easily slipped into a pre-dug shape. Pre-fabricated fibreglass liners can be the simplest – and usually the cheapest – way to install a pond, but over time they will usually become brittle and possibly crack.

There is no denying that projects involving water are the most problematic of landscaping jobs and need careful consideration. Remember, too, that water is extremely heavy (1 tonne per cubic metre) and it will, of course, always find its own level. Put simply: there's no room for error! It may be worth calling in a professional.

above **Water lilies have a wonderful flower and their foliage helps to keep direct sunlight off the top of the water.**

below **These *Zantedeschia aethiopica* look great near water. They are in individual planting spaces and flower all summer long.**

PLANTING UP YOUR POND

It is essential to achieve the correct balance of plants in your pond. They will ensure you have good quality water – dirty or cloudy water is not going to look good whatever style of garden you have. You *can* buy filtration systems and if the water is regularly moving this will also help to oxygenate it, but it is far better to achieve this naturally through good planting.

In spring, sun hitting the surface of the water encourages algae to grow, which will turn the water green. All ponds go a bit green in the spring, but if they're healthy they will clear up quickly. Partially covering the surface of your pond with plants can help keep sunlight off the surface, preventing some of the algae growth. This has the added benefit of creating hiding places for fish.

Try to integrate the edge of the pool into its surrounding and conceal its liner. Consider creating a 'soft' edge with plenty of planting – you may want to build a shelf below the surface of the water to stand marginal plants on.

Water plants are basically split into three groups: oxygenators, marginals and aquatics.

OXYGENATORS

These are fully submersed and will really help to keep the water clear. *Elodea crispa* and *Ceratophyllum demersum* are two of the most reliable and quick-spreading oxygenators. When you buy them, they generally come with small weights attached so that they immediately sink to the bottom of a pond.

MARGINALS

Good examples to use include *Typha minima*, which is a dwarf bulrush with a stiff upright stem and strong simple outline (like the larger bulrush, but smaller); the Arum lily (*Zantedeschia aethiopica*), a reliable, stately plant with an unmistakable, classic creamy-white spathe in early summer; and *Sagittaria sagittifolia*, which has elegant, arrow-shaped leaves and quickly forms dense clumps. Loose clusters of white three-petalled flowers appear as an added bonus in mid to late summer.

AQUATICS

There are many fabulous aquatic water lilies, but most of them grow too big for a small pond. Look for small varieties, such as *Nymphaea* 'Marliacea Rosea'. It's a compact grower with intense pink, fragrant blooms among purple-green leaves. The sweetly scented water hawthorn *Aponogeton distachyos* is also a good aquatic in city ponds.

scent: intoxicate

Scent is a very important part of the stress-busting garden. A plant's perfume is fragrance in its most natural and purest of forms and it can really help to make a city garden feel complete. With careful selection, it's possible to create a garden filled with year-round scent, which can trigger memories, evoke specific moods and help to relax the mind.

There is a vast range of aromas available in the plant world, from powerful, heady roses through the sweeter jasmines to the spicy clove-scented pinks. Scent is also very subjective and our personal associations through smell are complex, with some people loving aromas that others might loathe.

In the evening, as the light fades, a plant's scent becomes more important than its visual qualities. It is, therefore, important to position scented plants where they can be used to best effect – around seating areas or near to the back door of the house or apartment.

It is usually in the late spring and summer, when we spend a greater amount of time outside, that scented plants become essential to a small garden. There are, however, many winter and early spring flowering scented plants, though these may be better placed in the front garden, where they will be passed daily and fully appreciated.

AROMATIC FOLIAGE

It's not only the flowers of a plant that can be scented. Aromatic foliage can be surprisingly pungent. Lavender and rosemary are unbeatable for filling the city garden with an unmistakable Mediterranean scent. There are plenty of other herbs with aromatic foliage, too, which can be picked and thrown straight onto the barbecue. Fennel is a beautiful garden plant, which can reach over 2m high and can therefore help to add real height to your garden, as well as its aniseed scent. Sage is easy to grow in a pot or over the side of a raised planter. All forms of mint have a strong smell, as does the Sweet

bay (*Laurus nobilis*), which doubles up as a good evergreen hedge. The Katsura tree (*Cercidiphyllum japonicum*) is a great tree for a small garden and in the autumn, as the leaves decay on the ground, they give off the delicious smell of caramel or burnt sugar.

This clump of *Verbena bonariensis* will not only look good, flowering for many months, but also attract butterflies and bees into the garden all summer long.

BUTTERFLIES AND INSECTS

Scented plants are not only for our benefit, they have developed their strong scent specifically to attract pollinating insects. Therefore, they can help form the basis of a wildlife haven for bees and butterflies.

Scented plants such as *Buddleja*, *Escallonia*, *Verbena bonariensis* and *Helianthus*, as well as many native trees and shrubs, provide essential food for butterflies and bees. So, plant a combination of these (and those on the following pages), sit back, wait and watch.

evening plants and butterfly attractors

Annuals

Matthiola bicornis (Night-scented stock)
This is easy to grow and its mauve, pink or purple flowers are highly perfumed at night, so make sure to plant it near to paths and seating areas.

Nicotiana sylvestris (Tobacco plant)
A tall, classy plant with large sprays of drooping white flowers with an intense scent throughout the day.

Oenothera biennis (Evening primrose)
Plants can reach quite a height – up to 1.5m. It has cheery yellow, scented flowers, which open up in the evening and attract moths.

Perennials

Hesperis matronalis (Sweet rocket)
Deliciously scented pale lilac flowers in early summer above rosettes of dark green leaves. Great for attracting wildlife.

Phlox
Good old-fashioned cottage garden plants, which can also work well in a sunny or partially shady spot in a city garden. They have a lovely sweet perfume.

Erysimum cheiri (Wallflower)
Available in a range of great colours. They will flower from late winter right through to early autumn and have a strong, spicy scent.

left **Tobacco plants and buddleja are two plants that will fill your garden with wonderful scent. Of course, you can incorporate lovely smells into any style of garden be it formal or more naturalistic.**

Bulbs and corms

Narcissus (Daffodil)
There are loads of easy to grow daffodils that can either be grown outdoors or forced indoors for a good scent in early spring.

Lilium (Lily)
The *longiflorum* and *regale* lilies are the most powerfully scented varieties. They are blowsy plants that may look best grown in a pot.

Hyacinthus davidii (Hyacinth)
Delicately scented and available in a good range of colours. 'Woodstock' has deep magenta blooms for a more sophisticated look.

Shrubs

Buddleja davidii (Butterfly bush)
A magnet for butterflies, as its name suggests. Flowers in mid summer with long honey-scented flowers. Can be pruned to any height. 'Black Knight' has dramatic dark purple flowers.

Clerodendron trichotomum (Clerodendrum)
A tree-like shrub that can reach 3m high and is perfect for the city garden. Has intoxicating white blooms in late summer.

Lavandula angustifolia 'Hidcote'
A lovely compact lavender with deep violet flowers and aromatic foliage, perfect for edging paths.

Climbers

Lonicera periclymenum 'Serotina' (Honeysuckle)
This twining honeysuckle has creamy white flowers in mid-June with an orange-red streak and a classic honeysuckle scent.

Jasminum officinale (Jasmine)
One of my favourite summer smells. Although a little unruly, a single plant can fill a small garden with its perfume.

Trachelospermum jasminoides (Star jasmine)
A useful evergreen climber with small white flowers and a strong jasmine-like scent. Will grow well in sun or shade.

Exotics

Datura and *Brugmansia* (Angel's trumpet)
Large trumpet-shaped, sweetly scented flowers mainly in pink or white varieties. They open up at night and remain open until the morning.

Gardenia jasminoides (Cape jasmine)
This evergreen shrub has large white flowers with a fabulous exotic fragrance. Half hardy so grow in a large pot indoors and move out for the summer.

Citrus
Plants such as lemons, oranges, limes and kumquats all have amazing fresh and zingy scented flowers, but you'll need a cool conservatory or greenhouse to overwinter them in as they hate central heating.

Winter scent

Lonicera x *purpusii* 'Winter Beauty' (Shrubby honeysuckle)
The clusters of pale yellow tubular flowers pack a punch with their strong heady fragrance. Flowers in late winter and early spring. You'll need a bit of space, as it can grow to about 2m in both height and spread.

Chimonanthus praecox (Wintersweet)
This vigorous shrub certainly lives up to its name with heavenly scented, pale yellow flowers on bare stems. Established plants will flower all winter.

Viburnum x *bodnantense* 'Dawn' and 'Charles Lamont'
These both have amazing scented clusters of pink flowers on deeper pink bare stems. Blooms in autumn and winter.

outdoor living

opposite **This highly designed garden was planned almost entirely around the garden furniture to make it very much an outdoor room. The timber of the furniture relates well to the timber deck creating an homogenous look.**

left **Be realistic about how many people you'll get round a table without it feeling too cramped. This balcony is just right for a couple to have a drink or breakfast together, but simply wouldn't work with a formal dining table.**

The tools that enable you to turn your garden into an outside living space — such as lighting and furniture — will also help style and define its character. Most of these items can be bought *ad hoc* after the basic garden layout has been completed, which leaves room for an impulse buy or two. But do be careful, as you can end up regretting not making some key decisions earlier on. For example, you may have wished that you had known exactly what sized table and chairs you were going to incorporate, as the ones you want now don't quite fit, or, even worse, that they won't even get through the front door when the delivery arrives! (Oh yes, I've seen that one.) Wherever possible plan ahead.

When designing gardens for my clients I always find out how they want to use their garden and how they entertain, as the garden has increasingly become a place to enjoy with friends. Do they have regular and relatively formal dinner parties? And, if so, is the garden the place for a full-on dining table? Or will it be for just a few pre-dinner drinks before heading indoors? Or perhaps they entertain in a more relaxed manner with other families coming over for the day, and therefore want the garden to be flexible enough to seat larger numbers, but dotted throughout the garden. These decisions all help to build up a profile of how the garden will and can be used, and will relate back to the main design layout.

How the rooms at the back of the house are laid out and the way that they lead onto the garden will also have a role to play here. If the kitchen connects straight to the garden, people will move from one to the other and use the kitchen for food preparation and cooking, whereas if the kitchen is further away it's more likely that everything will be carried down in one go and the need for additional tables and a barbecue is greater.

Permanent installations, such as lighting, will need careful pre-planning ahead of any initial construction with regard to the positioning of electricity cables and switches.

furniture

Although good garden furniture can start to get expensive, it will instantly visually 'upgrade' an otherwise pretty average garden. Cheap-looking furniture will have precisely the opposite effect and is often the first place the eye comes to rest in small garden.

There are hundreds of different types and styles available to buy, some made entirely from wood and some a combination of wood and metal – such as lightweight aluminium. Other materials that are now widely used include woven rattan and wicker, synthetic woven materials, plastic and acrylics.

If you are creating a contemporary garden, avoid introducing traditional furniture, and look for a style that will work with the garden as a whole. Avoid white garden furniture as it is an extremely demanding colour and rarely compliments any other structures or planting in a garden.

DINING TABLES AND CHAIRS

Some small gardens have been completely designed around a main table and a set of chairs to create the ultimate 'outdoor dining room'. As with interior tables, consider extendible ones that will give you increased flexibility. Round tables work well where space is short.

SOFAS

With the demand for comfort, some companies are producing sofas similar to interior living-room furniture with shower-proof cushions. You can buy them in modules that can be moved around into different arrangements, providing a far more relaxed seating solution to the garden, but they are usually bulky items that will dominate a space.

STEAMERS/LOUNGERS

Steamers and loungers tend to be for those who take their relaxation as horizontally as possible, or are total sun worshippers. They do tend to take up a lot of space, but then I suppose it is your garden! Some will fold smaller than others when not in use, which will have a bearing on where they can be stored.

AL FRESCO EATING
Garden centres and interior furniture shops now sell a range of foldable café-style tables and chairs. These are ideal for tiny gardens and balconies for breakfasting in a sunny spot. You can also add them to existing seating areas to create more space for entertaining.

HAMMOCKS
There is nothing better than relaxing and swinging in a hammock under the shade of a tree on a hot summer's day. Some hammocks come attached to frames, while others will need strong fixings built into the walls, or you could tie them around a couple of mature trees in a more traditional manner. The ones without frames can easily be rolled up and stored away for the winter, so consider whether you want a hammock frame taking up a large chunk of your garden all year round. I prefer the Mexican-style hammocks, which you lie sideways in; the larger ones will take the whole family. They do, however, need more space than you think: around 3.5-4m between fixings.

WINTER STORAGE
When buying furniture, think about where and how it will be stored during the winter months. Some furniture can be left outside, uncovered all year, whereas wooden furniture ideally needs covering to increase its lifespan. Maybe it could be lifted and stored out of sight? Otherwise, you'll be looking at a covered table and chairs right through the winter.

CUSHIONS, BEAN BAGS AND CHILL-OUT MATS
It's great to be able to transform a space by throwing down mats and cushions onto the terrace, deck or lawn to lie on. As well as the more traditional Eastern-style mats, there are many new products that have been developed specifically for the garden. Most of them are made from easy-to-clean, water-resistant fabrics, but they shouldn't be left out all the time as they will deteriorate and get dirty. You can also buy interlocking rubber tiles that can be put down to soften a hard surface to make a softer children's play area or to make an ideal spot for a stretch and a bit of yoga.

BENCHES
Benches help to define and hold a particular area of the garden together when placed under a tree, say, or onto a planted gravel surface. Try to avoid benches that would look more at home in a park and see it as an opportunity to add in a more sculptural element. Maybe you could make something yourself? Or commission a carpenter to make something bespoke?

BUILT-IN
Built-in furniture can work extremely well in a garden, as it will become a strong permanent visual feature. Build it out of complementary or matching materials to fully integrate it. If any retaining walls are to be built, these can form the back of a bench, making built-in furniture an efficient use of space. An L-shaped bench works well where space is limited, and is a sociable set-up. An additional table and a few extra chairs can be brought in when needed to complete the arrangement. The big consideration with built-in furniture is comfort. When designing your furniture consider introducing fitted cushions, and allow the appropriate extra space.

If you really want to be able to use your garden as the main stress-busting room of the house and maximise its potential use and visual value throughout the year, then lighting in some form or other is essential.

On summer evenings lighting will transform your garden into a magical place, one that is very different from the daytime, and it will certainly extend the hours you will want to stay outside. Through the early spring, autumn and winter months when the days are short, garden lighting will draw your eye through that otherwise depressing, dark reflective window, and transform your garden into an ever-changing picture from inside the house.

When key plants are lit at night their individual characteristics are highlighted in interesting new ways. Sculptural plants such as *Agaves* and *Yuccas* become stronger forms when they are picked out with a spotlight or shown in silhouette, whilst the translucent leaves of some plants, such as red *Acers* or bananas, hold the light particularly well when back-lit. By lighting ponds or level changes and throwing spotlights over dining areas you will make your garden a safer and more usable space in the evenings, too.

lighting

above **The fluorescent lighting set into the ground can be walked on during the day and adds a real wow factor to the garden at night. As well as emphasising the strong layout it throws an interesting ambient blue light onto the timber seats.**

left **'Shadowing' is a simple technique where a cleverly placed spotlight will throw a silhouette shadow of a plant or a feature onto a wall.**

DIRT CHEAP
The only lights that don't need a qualified electrician to install are low voltage or solar-light systems that often come in kits from DIY stores. Solar is fine for a little ambient lighting at dusk, but will quickly fade, whereas low-voltage kits, although dimmer than mains voltage, are pretty effective for their cost and are very safe.
By combining candle lighting and low voltage you can make some exciting, adaptable compositions.

MEDIUM PRICE
A local landscaping company or qualified creative electrician can help you with some lighting design ideas and install a simple lighting system using mid-range fittings. Give yourself flexibility with lengths of cables, especially in planting areas, so that you can move lights around. If retro-fitting an existing garden, avoid lifting expanses of paving to lay cables. Make sure to get a certificate from the electrician once finished.

HIGH SPEC
Lighting designers will design and install a bespoke lighting scheme using top-of-the-range fixtures. They can set it up on various circuits giving you the option of various lighting combinations, all operational from a single remote control. This sort of system is usually built in during landscape works and often fittings are set into elements of hard landscaping or water so try and plan well ahead.

lighting effects

The most important thing to remember with lighting is the subject matter that you are trying to highlight. I have seen too many lights set into paving and decks that serve very little purpose, apart from lighting the air above them. Often the functional qualities of lighting in a garden – such as indicating where level changes, steps and paths are – will help define the garden's structure at night, and these can be supplemented with more creative lighting. Lights can be fixed to trees and walls to throw down light onto terraces and eating areas, for example.

With all forms of lighting, it's important to angle the source correctly, so that it doesn't glare and distract you when you look towards it. If possible, have the lights installed with two or three brightness levels, so that the lights can relate to your specific needs.

Garden lighting can also increase security, but specific security lighting that operates by sensors can be extremely irritating for you and your neighbours, as passing cats often set them off. Pretty much any type of garden lighting will work as a deterrent.

SPOTLIGHTING
Highlights a particular plant or feature, such as a sculpture. It will create a dramatic effect, drawing the eye towards whatever is being lit, and should ideally be viewed from a reasonable distance, otherwise it can appear too harsh.

UPLIGHTING
Used to light the crown of a particular tree or large shrub. The light is set at ground level and points upwards to illuminate the branches against the night sky or dark background. This technique can also be used on structures such as archways and pergolas. It really helps to keep the height in the garden and is very atmospheric.

GRAZING
This technique is mainly used to light walls and hard landscaping structures. Lights are positioned to show off a particular surface or structure, such as the texture of bricks in a wall or the slats in a fence. If the subject is painted, then this method of lighting will also bring ambient colour into the garden, which I find is far more successful than using coloured lights, which tend to look garish and distort the existing colours of the garden. Grazing lights will also help to keep the structure of the garden visible at night, important if you want to avoid your garden feeling overly 'soft'.

DOWNLIGHTING
This can highlight either the crown of a tree or a specific area of your garden from above. A series of lights set into the branches of a tree will imitate the effect of a strong moon and will provide a general outline of the tree. Downlighters that have been set into a tree or fixed to a wall can be specifically directed to create pools of light on certain areas of the garden, to reveal its layout or highlight features, such as the path through an arch.

UNDERWATER LIGHTING
Waterproof lights can be placed under the water in ponds or fountains. These lights will give the whole water feature a glow and will emphasise any movement on its surface. The underwater lighting of a waterfall or fountain can create a very dramatic effect and turn the waterfall into a cascade of light.

SILHOUETTING AND SHADOWING
Lighting a plant or sculpture from the front will cast a theatrical shadow onto the wall behind it. The shadow will change according to the size of the object, the distance between the light and its subject matter and the intensity of the light. The light fitting should be completely hidden to achieve maximum effect.

This is a very well designed and integrated lighting system
that was planned into the garden at a very early stage.
It balances out both the hard and soft landscaping whilst
bringing out the form, colour and detail of the palms and
bamboo beautifully.

the family garden

Rather than turning your family garden into a kids' playground look to make the areas as flexible as possible for a variety of uses.

The garden has always been a safe, contained environment for kids to play in, without their parents worrying where they are or what they're up to.

A garden for play needs to be tough and able to cope with the occasional trampling and the odd ball being thrown into the plants. To a degree this will have affected your choice of plants for the garden, but they may need updating over time as the way your children use the space changes. You can't be too precious in a family garden and you will simply have to accept that it will get battered every

now and then. Also, remember that children grow up frighteningly fast, get bored playing with the same old stuff and what they may have enjoyed last year is now not for them.

Rather than installing expensive specialist play equipment that will completely dominate the look of your garden, view the garden layout as a route for them to play along, with the option to jump on and off low walls, run through a path between some tall planting and try to include somewhere to hide, maybe a den, where they can do their own thing away from their parents' prying eyes.

CLIMBING FRAMES

Often the first choice is a climbing frame that comes in a kit. But consider building a pergola structure that can be adapted and integrated into the garden at a later stage. The surfacing under and around the structure needs to be considered, either using loose bark or rubber tiles designed precisely for this purpose.

OUTDOOR POOLS AND PADDLING POOLS

There are some great inflatable paddling pools and even small swimming pools available now. The larger ones come complete with their own filtration systems. They are fairly easy to install, but will need perfectly level ground. And, of course, there are major safety issues with water of any depth.

TRAMPOLINES

Trampolines are becoming increasingly popular, and are good fun and great exercise for the whole family. You can buy the trampoline on its own, or with a tall cage-like protection net for extra safety, which is advisable, as they can be pretty dangerous for small children. It is quite a hassle to put them up and take them down, so think about putting them up for the spring and summer and dismantling them over winter.

FAMILY GAMES

There are plenty of garden games available these days, including skittles, building blocks and boules/petanque. Think about the size of space and the garden surfaces you have before you make your purchase. You will need a gravel surface, ideally quite compacted, for boules, but a hard, level surface for skittles. You can adapt these games easily or make up your own.

TABLE TENNIS AND BADMINTON

These are best played in a sheltered garden. Outdoor table tennis tables can be folded upright, wheeled around and stored away easily. When set up they do need plenty of space around them to play without restriction. Badminton can be played by simply tying a proper net or even just a piece of string from between a couple of trees or fence posts. But be careful of losing the shuttlecock over the fence!

There's no doubt that the smaller your garden is, the more creative you have to be with the space available, and I have already stressed that limited space needs increased flexibility. With a little thought, the main surfaces can be quickly cleared and turned into temporary play areas for table tennis or boules, for example, and then turned back into dining or seating areas for entertaining and relaxing. But if football and cricket are going to be played on a regular basis then the local park is probably a better option.

eating out

When the weather's good it is time to enjoy and take full advantage of your city garden. There's nothing quite like eating and drinking in the open air and there's something about eating in my garden that makes me feel especially privileged that I have my own private outside space. On a sunny morning I love to take some toast and a fresh cup of coffee into the garden to set me up before work, and if it's a weekend I'll sit there with the paper and get away with doing as little as possible for as long as possible!

A lazy day spent in the garden that slips into a warm, balmy evening creates the perfect opportunity to invite friends round for an impromptu gathering with plenty of food and drink. I bring out extra chairs and cushions from inside if needed and throw beanbags around for an informal, relaxed setting. You may, however, prefer a more formal outdoor dining space, which will need more planning and thought in the initial design layout.

When the weather is fine, preparing food in the garden puts a fun emphasis on what can otherwise be a mundane indoor chore. I always find cooking outdoors hugely pleasurable and there are plenty of products available now to make it easy to do, whether you go for a fully loaded outside kitchen, a built-in wood-fired pizza oven, or a simple throw-away barbecue.

BARBECUES
Although I'm often asked to build a barbecue into the garden, I try to avoid doing so, as they don't tend to look great, have a habit of collecting debris and can't be stored away when not in use. Free-standing ones seem to cook better, are easier to clean and are better value for money. They can also be changed or upgraded more easily. Storage is an issue, so think about where they'll go when they're not being used over the winter. Some people

(usually men with a beer in one hand!) see themselves as Barbecue Kings and swear by their preference of either gas or charcoal. I'd say it depends on how you prefer the food to taste. But remember, if you do have a charcoal barbecue, to get it going long before anyone hungry turns up, to avoid disappointment.

OUTDOOR KITCHENS
Over the years the humble barbecue has morphed into a more sophisticated all-singing, all-dancing outdoor kitchen, which often comes complete with oven, fridge and worktops. If you take your cooking seriously, then look into installing one of these, but it will need careful thought to work with the garden as a whole, as they can easily overly dominate a small garden.

FIRE PITS
A fire pit can be built into a garden at ground level and will make an interesting focus for a surrounding seating area, and for the garden as a whole. It can be used for cooking and will also heat a surprisingly large area. If you are sinking it below ground level, consider how the water will drain away when it rains. (Note that the fuel you burn will depend on local guidelines.)

SHADES AND PARASOLS
There are very few who like to sit and lunch in the full sun. Look to create dining areas where you already have natural shade in the garden – under a tree or near a wall – or consider temporary awnings, shades and parasols, which can be put up and taken down easily.

HEATERS
Gas-fired heaters may extend the hours that the garden can be used right into the autumn, but they are extremely inefficient and environmentally unsound as they churn out huge quantities of carbon dioxide emissions.

When the weather's good there's
simply nowhere better to eat
than in the garden. This dining
terrace was planned specifically
around a main table. The large
free-standing parasol creates
shade and increases privacy.

a roof terrace

Many city roofs are being converted into fabulous stress-busting roof terraces. Before you start any work, check with your local planning officer to ensure it can be officially used as a garden and consult a structural engineer to calculate the maximum weightload it can take. This will determine what materials and plants you can incorporate.

safety
Roof terraces require strict safety standards. Balustrades have to be installed professionally to the necessary height for obvious safety reasons. Although you may look to install the surfaces and planters yourself, this is one area that simply can't be skimped on.

raised beds
All the plants will need to be grown in containers and will need a strict watering regime to stop them drying out completely. Galvanised steel planters are an ideal choice, as they are lightweight, are available in any size and can be powder coated to add some colour to your design.

surfaces
When installing the surfaces on a roof terrace it's critical not to penetrate the sealed waterproofing layer. Timber, stone and gravel can all be installed onto a custom-made frame or use adjustable spacers to ensure free draining. This will stop the build-up of any water and, therefore, weight.

seating
These built-in benches help to break up the space without making it feel cluttered and are also generous enough to double up as loungers. Free-standing furniture is always difficult to tie down on roof terraces where strong winds are an issue so building it in is a safer bet.

planting
As all the plants are grown in containers you are restricted to those that thrive in relatively shallow soil and that can cope with drying winds and exposure to strong sun. Grasses and perennials are a great choice for impact during the summer when the roof terrace will mainly be used.

barrier
The choice of timber balustrades helps maintain the chunky look of this roof terrace. The dimensions of the actual boards visually ties them to the decking and seating, giving the whole garden a cohesive look. The solid boundary also makes the roof garden feel safer and more secure.

lighting
This garden uses a combination of lighting techniques. Spike lights have been set in the planters, which work alongside a series of LED lights under the frosted glass inserts set into the surfaces. Rope lights create the pink lines at the base of the planters.

JAZZING UP

freshening up the space

Most gardens benefit from a focussed injection of energy and creativity every now and then, and with a small city garden it's easy to make plenty of impact without breaking the bank – or your back. It may be that your garden is looking a little tired in between seasons and needs a splash of colour to see it through, or perhaps there's a key date in the diary that you need the garden to look special for, such as a birthday. If the weather forecast is looking good for the weekend, with a little effort the garden can become the ideal party venue.

I have worked on many garden makeover TV shows and, although they have received a bad press for rushed work and a superficial approach, many of the quick fixes we used considerably improved the style and look of the gardens we worked on. Sure, a really great garden will take time to develop, but it will also need a helping hand along the way to freshen it up and to keep it looking interesting – and stop you from losing interest in it. Jazzing up your garden will quickly turn round any negative feelings that you may have towards it. A big bonus of having a small garden is that it's easy to make a strong visual impact in just a few hours. Even short periods of time 'vamping' it up will spur you on to get more involved, and will ultimately lead to you getting far more out of your garden in the long run.

If you are renting your house or apartment you'll understandably be reluctant to splash out lots of cash on any permanent planting or structures, but there are plenty of quick-fix solutions that'll make it look more inviting and there are some decorative elements that you can take with you when you leave – just like the pictures on the walls in the hallway. If you own the property, but are looking to sell, there is no doubt that a smart garden can help swing it in your favour with prospective buyers.

A lick of paint here and there along with the odd piece of temporary screening will help divert the eye away from any major negatives in the garden and upgrade the overall look. Seasonal planting can be added in and regularly updated through planting up containers or by sorting out weaker spots in the permanent planting. If you can plan ahead, then bulbs can go into the ground in the autumn for a spring display, but if you miss the boat, most of them are available as pot-grown plants coming into bud in the spring. Pot-grown bulbs and annuals *are* more expensive, but using them gives you scope to play around with the composition, rather than having to visualise how they will come up together.

A property with any outside space in the city is a huge draw, so a weekend spent giving it a once over and jazzing it up could make all the difference. I bet you won't lose out on any time or money you invest.

As well as creating instant shade and privacy, sail shades help style the overall garden and provide a 'ceiling', increasing the sense of seclusion. If the weather forecast is good why not take interior cushions and chairs outside to complete the look?

Succulent plants, such as this flowering *Aloe*, are drought tolerant and therefore
extremely low maintenance as they need little watering. They should be overwintered
in a greenhouse or conservatory, but can be left out in the garden all summer long.

Containers and pots are ideal for keeping your garden looking fresh throughout the whole year and they can be great fun to plant up and play around with. See them as styling accessories that can be moved, changed and experimented with and don't get too hung up on trying to make them overly 'tasteful', or else your garden will end up looking like the pub down the road!

If your garden is paved over, or you are gardening on a balcony or rooftop, containers may be the only planting space you have. Whatever the style of container you go for, make sure that they are as large as possible for their allotted space. Plants don't tend to like mean little pots, as they cramp their roots, dry out quickly and often look completely out of scale even in the smallest of gardens. Think about lifting the pots up on blocks or plinths nearer to eye level, too, rather than placing them all on the ground.

Most grasses, perennials and many small shrubs, such as azaleas, *Sarcococca* (Christmas box), *Viburnum davidii* (Viburnum) and the striking purple-berried *Callicarpa bodinieri* (Beautyberry), all look great started off in a container for a seasonal hit of colour. They can then be planted out into the garden in a permanent spot. Architectural plants and exotics will add plenty of sculptural form, but if you want plenty of colour then annuals will give you everything they can all summer long.

BULBS

Bulbs are little capsules of stored energy that can be planted in pots to flower wherever you want, and in either sun or shade. They can be combined with other plants, such as wallflowers, or try planting them in layers in containers. Plant some tulips at the bottom, narcissi in the middle and then the smallest and first to flower, such as crocus and *Iris reticulata*, on the top for a succession of flowers from early to late spring. For around six weeks after they've flowered they will need some sunlight on their foliage if they are to flower the next year, and once they've died back they can be transplanted into the garden to naturalise.

ANNUALS AND PERENNIALS

Annuals and tender perennials are the archetypal container plants, enjoying the well-drained conditions that a pot has to offer. They fill the garden with colour from early summer right through until the first frosts. *Petunia*, *Cosmos*, *Pelargonium* (Geranium), *Impatiens*, *Anemone* x *hybrida* (Japanese anemone), *Nicotiana* (Tobacco plant), *Osteospermum* and *Tropaeolum* (Nasturtium) are just a few of the huge range of plants to choose from. These can be put together in either subtle or crazy colour combinations depending on your tastes. Make sure that you deadhead these plants regularly to keep new flower buds coming through.

ALPINES

Alpines such as *Armeria maritima* (Sea pink), *Arabis* (Rock cress), alpine Phlox and *Saxifrage* will thrive in containers. They combine well together and will provide low, evergreen cushions of foliage and pretty flowers from late spring to early summer. They can be left in all year round for the ultimate in low maintenance gardening.

SUCCULENTS AND CACTI

Succulents and specialist plants, such as *Echeveria*, *Sedum*, *Agave*, *Aloe* and *Yucca*, grown in pots will give the garden an arid, foreign look. They aren't fond of the cold, although in protected areas some will survive outdoors through the winter. They can also be grown indoors, or in a conservatory, and taken into the garden for the summer to temporarily transform a particular area.

WINTER SOLUTIONS

During the winter we all need a shot of colour in our lives. Plants such as flowering *Cyclamen* and heather and the berrying *Skimmia* can be combined with foliage plants such as Ivy, *Euonymus* and the dramatic black Lily Grass for some really interesting combinations to help see your garden through.

filling in the gaps

The decision to paint the chair bright pink came from the floriferous *Geranium* 'Anne Thomson'. The mass planting of the frothy acid green *Alchemilla mollis* and red *Astrantia* completes the strong summer display.

Empty and poorly planted areas of your garden can be a real let-down and, in my view, large expanses of soil left bare are both depressing and a missed opportunity. For some totally unfathomable reason there are people who like to see distinct areas of clear soil in between their plants, as if this keeps them organised and compartmentalised. But dark soil, especially in a shady city garden, is not the best material to show off plants, and it will only encourage weeds and increase maintenance in the long run. Sure, there will be times when areas will be bare, but look to fill every available planting space at every opportunity and try to really cram in the plants, which may just be a case of lifting and dividing any perennials that you already have and putting them back in the gaps.

HARDY ANNUAL SEED MIXES

A rough piece of ground in a sunny spot can easily be dug over, raked and sown directly with inexpensive packet seed. Hardy annuals such as cerinthe, Love-in-a-mist, poppies, nasturtiums and cornflowers can be sown in late summer or early spring for a colourful display all summer long. There are plenty of pre-mixed combinations available in packets or make up a mix of your own. Make sure to sow them thinly and then thin them out as they grow to give each plant some space.

SELF-SEEDED PLANTS

Plants such as *Alchemilla mollis* (Lady's mantle), *Euphorbia* (Spurge) and fennel, and many ornamental grasses along with biennials

This combination of grasses, succulents and herbs needs minimal watering. The large leaves of the *Paulownia tomentosa* make a dramatic statement and can be kept at the required height by coppicing annually.

such as foxgloves and honesty will freely sow themselves around your garden, especially in loose gravel areas. To cover any bare patches, carefully lift and transplant these seedlings – plants for free can't be bad!

TRICKY GAPS BETWEEN THE SEASONS

In most gardens, there will be certain times of the year, such as late summer and early autumn, when nothing is really flowering and it seems as if everything has finished for the year. Perennial plants such as Japanese anemones and asters are invaluable during this time, as they flower late in the year. And annual climbers, like the *Ipomoea lobata* (Spanish flag) and the purple *Ipomoea purpurea* 'Purple Haze' (Morning glory) can just

go on and on, way into the autumn, before they get knocked back by a frost.

SALADS

Another way to add to your seasonal planting through the summer and into autumn is to introduce, between the permanent planting, some salad plants. They certainly don't have to be in their own designated area and will grow very happily alongside ornamental plants. Cut-and-come-again lettuces, rather than the heart-forming varieties, are your best bet, as they can be cropped without having to dig up the entire plant and leave behind a big hole. Other good salad plants to squeeze into gaps are onions and chicory, and salad herbs such as rocket, basil, chives and coriander.

colour through paint and stains

Painted surfaces will introduce permanent colour into your garden, which will completely change its mood throughout the year. If lighting is also incorporated, it will bring colour into the garden at night as well, which is often absent, as plants don't usually have enough depth of colour to stand out in low light levels.

The right choice of colour and tone will make a huge impact on your outdoor area, and can convert a dark, dingy garden into a vibrant space. It's fairly easy to apply paints and stains to existing structures, such as fences, sheds, pergolas and walls – and even on ground surfaces – as well as to pots and containers. And, in addition to bringing

immediate colour directly into the garden, it's interesting to see how plants react to certain colours as a backdrop. Coloured walls often intensify the different greens in a garden and will draw attention to any coloured streaks or spots on the foliage. Coloured backgrounds will also show off the form of the flowers and exaggerate their colouring.

When introducing colour, use stains on timber and paint on masonry and rendered walls. Stains that soak into wooden materials are far easier than paint to re-apply in a few years, as the paint will have peeled off the wood in parts and so plenty of preparation will be needed before a new coat is put on.

The great thing about using strong colours, such as this red oxide painted wall, is that they intensify the greens of the foliage within the garden. Of course, if you want a change, paint can easily be re-applied to instantly change the mood of the garden.

PAINTING SURFACES

If you've inherited a garden with some awful concrete paving slabs or a poured concrete area, think about painting these, too. If they are uneven and cracked it's probably worth covering them with an aggregate *(see Quick Fix Solutions, page 157)*, but otherwise you can simply apply an outside floor paint. In the past, the colour range for outside floor paint has been extremely limited, but now some paint shops will mix you any colour you want. It's not a permanent solution and is not great for areas that receive lots of wear, but for a short period of time or for areas that are viewed more than used, such as dead ends and side alleys, it is an extremely effective way of bringing colour to your garden.

PAINTING CONTAINERS AND POTS

Pots and containers that are made from wood, stone or terracotta are pretty cheap to buy and can easily be jazzed up by painting them. Diluting the paint will create a wash, which will let some of the natural colour through, so look for earthy tones to complement it. Any pot that has a glaze is a bit trickier and is probably best avoided. Metallic containers can be painted with metal finish paint or, ideally, powder coated, which is not a DIY job.

WALLS AND FENCES

Ugly walls or fences, or at least key sections of them, can easily be clad in a different material to create an alternative feel and so 'lift' areas. Towards the back of a garden I will often use a waterproof ply-board to cover ugly bricks, creating a smooth finish, ready to take a couple of coats of masonry paint. Okay, so it's a quick fix that will last a few years rather than a permanent solution, but it certainly does the trick. If the garden has a valuable old brick boundary, it's often better to clean it up and re-point it rather than apply paint, which will be almost impossible to remove in the future.

WHICH COLOURS WORK WHERE

When you are choosing colours to paint or stain surfaces, it's worth going for a strong, simple theme and continuing it through a large part of the garden. Too many different colours will always look messy.

Blocks of bolder colours work extremely well, as they will intensify the greens of the plants and will give the garden a definite identity. Black can look wonderfully dramatic as a backdrop, but it does need plenty of green foliage to balance it out. Hotter colours, such as reds, oranges and earthy ochres, will keep the garden feeling warm throughout the year, whereas stronger blues, pinks and purples look great through the bright summer months, but will make the garden feel a degree or two cooler in the winter.

Light, natural colours such as creams, taupes, mushrooms and natural off-whites often work best in gardens, as they will bounce the light around even through the winter months. I find that they are also far easier to live with in the long term than a crazy pink or orange. Never use pure white in a garden, even in deep shade, as it is a very strong and demanding colour and is surprisingly difficult to combine with plants and other materials. Make sure that it always has a hint of something warmer in it to tone it down a touch.

If you aren't sure about colours and break into a sweat at the paint shop, get a few small sample pots and try them out – either directly onto the intended surface or onto a piece of board. And remember: you can always paint over it if you don't like it or become bored of it.

left This fence has been stained a light colour to work alongside the rendered wall. Together they really lift the back elevation of the garden. It's far easier to use a stain rather than paint on fences and trellis as it can be re-applied more easily.

above It's easy to make an impact in the garden by including colourful accessories, such as bright pots and furniture, rather than relying on the colour of flowers and foliage, which tends to be fleeting.

FURNITURE

Almost all garden furniture can be painted to give it a new lease on life and keep it working with your garden style. Even tired old wicker chairs will benefit from a lick of paint to squeeze another season out of them. But you shouldn't use large pieces of furniture to make a major statement with colour in your garden. If it is a well-designed, attractive piece of furniture then it will have intrinsic style and should be left alone, but if it's nothing special and you want to smarten it up, use a subdued colour; a strong one will only make it stand out and draw attention to it.

Smaller pieces of furniture, however, can be painted and used to brighten up a dull area of the garden. Treat them as accessories that can be moved about and updated regularly.

a garden room

bench seat
This large wooden bench with built-in back rest is long enough
to lie down on. When building or buying furniture, try to be as
generous as the space will allow, especially if you're looking to
use the garden for entertaining.

brazier
Fire pits are very
impressive and can be dug
below ground-level during
the garden construction
phase, but there is also a
wide choice of off-the-peg
accessories, such as this
brazier which will heat
part of the garden and
extend its use way into
the night.

planting style
Most cities will have a
protected microclimate,
which means that some
more exotic plants like
the sculptural tree fern
Dicksonia antarctica and
the evergreen loquat tree
will thrive. A few choice
large specimens will make
a considerable impact in a
garden whilst keeping the
sense of space.

Although this garden is really jazzed up, packed full of accessories and furniture,
it doesn't feel cluttered because the areas are generously sized and clearly
defined. The planting and lighting create an exotic holiday feel, ideal for chilling
out or partying.

screens

Bamboo and hazel screens
are economical and are
available in rolls. Many
people use them for
screening, but are
disappointed as they can
easily be seen through,
whereas here the partial
view adds plenty of
interest to the garden's
overall composition.

water feature

When introducing water
into the city garden
choose any off-the-peg
features carefully to
ensure that they sit
comfortably within the
style of the garden. This
simple dish style will
add sound and movement
to the garden both day
and night.

pebbles

As well as loose pebbles
and aggregates being one
of the easiest and cheapest
ways of covering ground,
they add plenty of texture,
too. In this case the choice
of white pebbles helps to
keep this shady garden
light throughout.

If you have people over regularly you simply can't have enough places to sit in the garden. This seating arrangement provides a relatively formal dining area and a less formal space, both in shade.

speedy updates

There are lots of ways to alter the look and style of your garden and to update or change it in a just a few hours. Think about how you might decorate your house and transfer these ideas to your outside space. You might have a children's party during the day and a dinner for friends in the evening, but with a few choice items you can go seamlessly from one into the next.

GARDEN DECORATION

There are so many ways to bring temporary decoration into your garden, from candle-holders and decorative pots to wall sculptures and plant supports. When looking to add extra decoration – whether to help a corner of the garden along or to add a feature to a bleak wall – make sure that what you choose is in proportion and in keeping with the overall style of the garden. Be ruthless and picky. Just because you've been given a Japanese lantern as a present doesn't mean it'll look great in your garden, in fact it's likely to be the most distracting thing in the garden. Be sparing with decoration and try to keep it simple, which may mean leaving out any DIY mosaics, unless you are particularly talented!

FABRICS AND CUSHIONS

Fabrics can be used to brighten up the garden and give it a one-off party look. You can completely cover existing structures such as pergolas and walkways or use them as an anchor to run a length of cord to another fixed point and drape fabric over it. A large sheet of fabric and a few clothes pegs will help to create extra privacy and shade, as well as introducing a decorative element. Outdoor cushions can be made to any size, and, as well as styling and making existing furniture more comfy, they can be used on low walls to increase the amount of seating in a garden. Although they are usually shower-proof, it's best not to leave them outside when not in use, so consider where they will be stored.

CUT FLOWERS AND POTTED PLANTS

When I talk about introducing cut flowers into the garden I don't mean trying to cheat by sticking them into flowerbeds as though you've grown them yourself! For parties and other gatherings, a few jugs or vases packed full of flowers and foliage and placed in key positions will focus the composition and help set the scene. You can buy them from your local florist, but there may be plenty of leaf, stem and flower material in your own garden already that can be supplemented with some bought ones.

TEMPORARY LIGHTS

In a similar way to using your interior furniture in the garden you could also use some interior lighting outside for a one-off temporary solution. In the past, I have run an extension cable into the garden and set up standard lamps and table lamps to help light the garden for a party. The effect was extremely effective with a fun and quirky twist. Of course, it's vital that the weather is dry with electrics being involved. And make sure to use a circuit breaker and tape down any loose cables.

Simple detailed touches, such as these tea lights in jars hanging between the gaps in the trellising, are so simple to do, but add a sense of fun to the evening garden and are also practical.

quick-fix solutions

Although it's better in the long run to take the time to correct any problem areas, sometimes a quick fix can solve the issue while you consider a more permanent option. Although short-term solutions are sometimes thought to be cheap looking and of poor quality, there are actually some very clever ways to sort out common garden complaints and spruce up an area that is looking a bit worse for wear.

SCREENING
Perhaps there's a part of the garden that's particularly unsightly and really lets the garden down overall, such as a play area, old shed or ugly wall. This can easily be screened off by putting up a visual barrier made from one of the natural materials like willow or heather that are now available in a roll. These make a fine temporary solution, but they quickly weather and decay and often don't form a full screen as they are usually partly see-through.

AWNINGS AND MARQUEES
I have been to parties where the entire garden has been covered with a marquee, bringing the garden plants into play in new and interesting ways to help form part of the now interior decoration. Some people invest in smaller,

This is the sort of garden that could be built in a couple of weekends, but will transform the way it's used and viewed. The wall, gravel and deck areas lay down the basic structure and the rest is simply styled with accessories: furniture, pots, a sculpture and some lights.

weight of your furniture combined with what access you have to the garden will determine whether it's worth the hassle or not.

LAWN FIXES
If you have a lawn in a small garden it may look a little the worse for wear, especially in the summer, but it can easily be re-turfed. If you are looking to re-lay a lawn for a party, then do it at least a month before to ensure that it is well bedded in. If the existing lawn is okay, then you can smarten it up by redefining the edge with a straight board and half-moon tool.

GRAVEL AND AGGREGATE SURFACES
Any loose surface pathways or garden areas laid with a loose material such as gravel or pebbles may benefit from being top dressed by simply spreading a few bags of the same material over the top. If you have a particularly grim looking concrete or paved area this could be dressed in a similar fashion to hide a multitude of sins, but make sure that there is an edge to retain the material. This could be just a simple piece of timber held in place with some wooden pegs.

MULCH
Mulching planting areas is mainly to suppress weeds, retain moisture and improve the soil, but it will also help to cover poor soil, and set off any plants that are managing to thrive. Composted bark, cocoa shell or leaf mould will all do the job. And whilst you're at it, mulch around the tops of any pots or containers to tie the look together.

PRESSURE WASH
Hard surfaces such as stone or deck flooring can quickly be cleaned up without the use of chemicals by using a pressure washer, and while you're at it spray down any furniture and pots, to make them look almost new. Be careful of washing out any loose pointing and grouting between paving.

expandable marquees and gazebos to try and beat the weather, as they work well to create shade on a hot sunny day as well as keeping things dry if there's an occasional shower.

TEMPORARY FURNITURE
If the weather forecast is good then why not think about turning your garden into the ultimate outside room? Interior furniture, such as sofas and armchairs, is designed for comfort and will help to transform your garden into a living room, ideal for a party. If you're worried about getting them dirty, cover them with an old blanket or throw. Of course, the size and

BLITZING

easy aftercare

A city garden shouldn't require lots of ongoing hard work or a 'Groundhog Day' list of mundane chores just to keep it looking good. This is where the careful planning you have done, bearing in mind the amount of maintenance time that will be available, really pays off. This will probably have affected some key design decisions along the way, such as surface finishes, proportion of plants to hard landscape and the types of plants you have chosen to grow. Ideally, your garden will also be able to cope with being neglected for lengthier periods of time without any long-term damage – if you're away on holiday, for example. Rather than being overly designed and too rigid, a garden, in my opinion, should give you the scope to add, take away and change some of its elements seasonally if you wish, or if you have a sudden surge of mad creativity on a sunny spring day, but maybe that's just me...

Of course, I'm a huge garden lover, but I am also pretty busy and away a lot, so I don't have lots of spare time at regular intervals. I certainly don't want my garden to become a burden to me and make me feel that I can't enjoy it properly without giving it a good once-over first. The more relaxed gardening approach of 'blitzing' every now and then works perfectly for me, and has certainly been a large factor in forming the style and feel of the garden, too. I blitz, more often than not, whenever it feels right, which is often a combination of when the weather's good and when I have the available time and energy to do it.

I have split the blitzing periods into the four seasons, but the climate across the country and the amount of protection a garden has can vary considerably. Some city gardens can go through mild winters without any frosts, and exotics and half-hardy plants can survive happily without any protection; in other cities if you want to grow these plants you'll need to be ready to move them into a conservatory or fleece them through the winter. Wherever you live, try to tune into the seasons, and be aware of the earliest and latest frosts in your garden as this will affect what you can grow and how to look after more sensitive plants.

Spring and autumn are the two main seasons when you will really need to get stuck in. At these times of year the garden can be edited – new plants can be put in and old ones pruned, lifted and moved. Don't rush into it in some crazed attack and chop everything back on the plants that have become a little overgrown. Most plants are pretty tough, but a degree or two of sound knowledge is certainly more important than blind enthusiasm. It's the experience and learning through success and failure that ultimately make a good gardener, and, in time, a particularly good garden.

I like to be as efficient as possible with my time and make sure that any time I do put into the garden is rewarded with seeing the fruits of my labour. Once you start

With good planning you can dictate precisely how much work will need doing.
This garden has minimal planting and needs very little ongoing maintenance,
apart from pruning the wisteria annually, but is still very much a 'garden'.

to build on your gardening experiences you will be able to speed things up and get through tasks quickly if you want to, which leaves more available time for new tasks, or for stress busting!

A purely organic approach to gardening is hard to implement in a small urban garden as organic material will need to be imported into the garden from time to time. I call myself an 'Easy Organic' gardener; I never use any chemical feeds or pesticides as healthy plants can usually fight off most pests and are resistant to diseases. If things get too bad I'd rather dig them up and start again than spray them all the time!

SPRING

Spring is the time to get outside and give your garden a really good going over in order to set it up for the year ahead. Wait for one of those brilliant fresh, sunny days to keep your spirits up and to help you to get the maximum enjoyment out of it. Give yourself enough time to deal with everything thoroughly, even if you have to leave parts of it and do it over two or three weekends. Any time you do put in now will pay you back in spades over the coming year.

Spring is the ideal time to see what is emerging in the garden with a view to filling in any gaps and balancing out the planting, whether that means buying in new plants or lifting and moving existing ones. As you work through the garden, keep standing back to get an overview of the space, looking at what you are doing with regard to the whole garden, as it is easy to get carried away in a particular corner without seeing the bigger picture. Try to visualise the impact of whatever changes you make now over the coming seasons.

SOIL AND MULCHING

■ If the soil isn't too wet, prepare it by digging it over and incorporating plenty of organic matter. This will reduce any compaction and get some air into it, making it easier to work with and plant into. Make sure to keep off the areas that you have already worked by standing on a board that has been laid on the earth.

■ If there are any perennial weeds hanging about from last year whose growing tips may have re-emerged, make sure to dig the entire root out. When the soil is weed-free and moist, mulch over the borders and around the plants with a generous layer of organic matter. This will help retain moisture in the soil throughout the year and will generally improve the quality of your soil. It will also help to feed your plants over the coming season.

■ Any plants that have been heavily pruned over the winter will appreciate a mulch to help stimulate new growth.

FEEDING

■ When the soil warms up and plants start to put on strong growth give them all a feed with a slow-release organic fertiliser.

BULBS AND PERENNIALS

■ Lift and divide clumps of snowdrops and winter aconites when they are still in leaf. Split them up carefully and replant them wherever desired.

■ Cut off the spent flower heads of *Narcissus* and tulips but wait a minimum of six weeks, until their foliage has died down, before removing it completely. Don't tie into silly knots like some people recommend!

■ Now is the time to plant dahlias and summer-flowering bulbs such as *Eremurus*, gladioli and *Eucomis*.

■ Ornamental grasses, which still have last year's foliage on, can be cut back hard, and lifted and divided if necessary. Be careful not

to damage the new shoots on any emerging new growth at the base.

■ Herbaceous perennials can still be lifted and divided if the soil is soft and workable (see Autumn for more details on this).

TREES, SHRUBS AND CLIMBERS

■ Take off any winter protection you may have put on, but keep an eye on the weather in case a late frost is forecast.

■ Check and adjust any tree ties that may now be too tight and any stakes that may have been blown around during the winter.

■ Continue or finish planting trees and shrubs early in the season. You can now also move around any existing evergreen shrubs.

■ Tie in climbers regularly to keep them tidy and to make sure they avoid any wind damage.

PRUNING

■ Early in the season, prune the late-flowering shrubs, such as *Caryopteris* x *clandonensis*, *Ceratostigma*, *Hydrangea paniculata*. Prune the more frost-sensitive shrubs, such as lavateras and many of the silver foliage shrubs, a little later in spring.

■ Prune back any spring-flowering shrubs such as forsythia and *Ribes* after flowering.

■ Shrubs such as *Buddleja davidii*, *Salix alba* var. *vitellina*, *Eucalyptus gunnii* and *Cornus sanguinea* cultivars can all be stooled, by cutting them back hard. This will keep them at a manageable size. It will also deepen the colour of their stem for those grown for an additional winter display.

■ If any variegated plants show signs of reverting to their natural green foliage, cut off the branch or stem right back to the point where it meets the main plant.

LAWNS

■ If the weather is favourable and the soil workable, now is a good time to lay a lawn using turf or by sowing seeds. Avoid walking on newly turfed areas for a few weeks in order to let the root system establish itself, and leave seeded lawns well alone until they have thickened up.

■ If you don't have a built mowing edge, straighten up the edges using a half-moon turf iron and a straight board. Using string, followed by a line of sand laid onto the ground as a guide, re-shape the arcs of curves.

■ Mow established lawns on a dry day as soon as the grass has started growing. Make sure to set your mower on its highest setting and slowly lower it over a few cuts.

■ In late spring, apply a high nitrogen organic feed to help green up your lawn.

PONDS AND WATER

■ Spring is a key time for pond maintenance. In late spring clean out dirty or overgrown ponds, but make sure to leave any vegetation by the side of the pond for at least a few hours, so that any wildlife can crawl back into the water. It's also a good time for lifting and dividing aquatic and marginal pond plants that have grown too large – in a similar way to overgrown garden perennials. City pond plants are usually planted into an aquatic basket using a low nutrient aquatic soil, so you may want to replace the soil.

■ It's also a good time to introduce new plants or even plant up a brand new pond. If you are making a new pond, incorporate a bucketful of established pond water from a friend's pond to speed up the balancing process and make it 'live'. Reinstate any pumps if you have taken them out for the winter.

SUMMER

In my opinion, the summer months are when an urban garden should be enjoyed and utilised as much as possible. The gardening aspect shouldn't consist of any serious graft, but be more a case of pottering about and doing the occasional tweaking. Jobs such as watering and deadheading shouldn't be rushed and, with a bit of practice, can be mastered with a drink in one hand!

MAIN JOBS

■ In early summer, plant up your containers for a summer display. Any plants that you may have moved into a greenhouse or conservatory over the winter can be brought outside now, if you haven't already done so, when there is no further fear of a frost.
■ Deadhead plants regularly to encourage new flower buds.

BULBS AND PERENNIALS

■ Lift and divide bearded iris as soon as they have finished flowering by lifting the whole plant, cutting into thirds with a sharp spade and replanting one third at a time.
■ Take softwood cuttings of half-hardy plants such as *Penstemons* and *Discias* as an insurance policy in case the ones in your garden don't make it through the following winter.
■ Start thinking about ordering bulbs to be planted in the autumn for a spring display.
■ Cut back some of the perennials that have finished flowering. Some plants such as perennial geraniums may reward you with a second flush later in the season.
■ Stake tall perennials to support them.

TREES AND CLIMBERS

■ Prune late-spring-flowering shrubs and climbers such as magnolia, lilac, philadelphus and deutzias once they have finished flowering.
■ Tie back any wispy growth from climbers such as wisteria, roses and honeysuckle.
■ Trim evergreen trees and hedges including shaping topiary.

LAWNS

■ In dry weather keep the mower on a high setting and leave clippings on the grass as a mulch to retain moisture. Continue to feed the lawn if it is still growing.

PONDS AND WATER

■ You can still clean out your pond in early summer. Thin out the leaves of water lilies and other pond plants if they have become too dense and top the pond up with water if it evaporates in the hot weather.

RAINWATER HARVESTING

■ With water becoming more expensive to buy, and the need for sustainable solutions all round, look to harvest and store any rainwater that falls in the footprint of your house and garden. Water butts attached to drainpipes are the simplest solution, but if you are laying a new terrace you could install a larger underground storage tank to collect the water that falls on the hard surface through a land drain.
■ Grey water from the shower and bath can't be stored, but it can be used immediately on the garden plants and lawn. Pump it out of the bath with a simple detachable pump, or use gravity to help distribute it. Water from the washing machine is too rich in detergents for the garden and waste water used for washing up or from the dishwasher will contain small food particles and is therefore best left as it may attract rodents into the garden.

HOLIDAY TIPS

■ If you go on holiday for a week or two, water any pots thoroughly and move them into a shady part of the garden.
■ If you have a children's paddling pool fill it with an inch or two of water and place the pots directly into it to stop them drying out.
■ Make sure to leave the planting areas weed free and well mulched to prevent any weeds getting a hold and competing with the plants for light and moisture.

AUTUMN

Autumn is the season to get into the garden and sort out any areas that are starting to look particularly messy after the summer, with a view to putting it to bed for the winter.

The ground is soft and the plants are fast approaching their dormant winter state, making it the ideal time for planting trees, shrubs and spring-flowering bulbs and for sorting out the lawn for the following year. In the past, gardeners have been overly keen to get the garden looking spick and span ready for the winter, cutting back perennials and picking up leaves the moment they drop as if there's somehow a rush. The problem with this approach is two-fold. Firstly, it's easy to miss out on the natural beauty of plants as they start to die back. Many plants, such as ornamental grasses, hold onto their foliage, whilst others have wonderful seed heads and twiggy habits that can look fantastic right through the winter, especially when they are frosted or back-lit by the low winter sun. Secondly, the city's ecosystem relies on these plants for the food and cover that they provide. There are plenty of birds and beneficial insects that like to forage under the leaves and which will lose out or move on if you tidy away their resource. My advice is slow down and let the garden dictate to you when anything needs to be done. If you are in any doubt, leave it a bit messy until your next spring blitz.

MAIN JOBS

■ Clear out any annual displays from pots and containers and plant them up with attractive winter combinations.

■ Clear away the fallen leaves from the main paving areas and lawns and make leaf mould (see page 167).

■ If you have any areas of heavy clay soil, dig it over and leave the larger clods of earth open to any winter frosts, which will help break them up for you.

BULBS AND PERENNIALS

■ Plant spring-flowering bulbs into the garden or in pots. Do this as soon as you buy them to stop the bulbs from drying out.

■ If you live in an area of heavy frosts, lift dahlias and other tender bulbs once the frost has blackened their leaves, knock off any loose soil and store them in a cool, frost-free environment over the winter. In milder areas you can leave them in the ground by cutting them to ground level, covering with a thick mulch and pinning a plastic sheet over the top of them to keep them dry and, hopefully, slug-free.

■ Lift, divide and re-plant perennials to create more plants and to rejuvenate plants whose centres are exhausted and have died out. With large clumps, dig up the entire plant and split it using garden forks placed back-to-back and then pushed apart. Sub-divide the plant further by cutting it into smaller pieces using an old serrated kitchen knife.

■ In late autumn mulch over half-hardy perennials.

TREES, SHRUBS AND CLIMBERS

■ Autumn is a good time for planting deciduous trees and shrubs as the dormant season is about to start. Nurseries will start selling bare-rooted trees and shrubs, which can work out better value for money and tend to perform more successfully in the long run.

■ Late autumn is also the best time to lift and move any existing trees and shrubs if they're not quite where you want them. Soak small shrubs a couple of days before you want to move them and prepare the new planting hole with plenty of organic matter.

■ If you have a newly landscaped garden, look to plant the framework in the autumn.

■ Many find pruning shrubs the hardest and scariest of gardening skills, but there really is nothing to be anxious about. In nature, plants don't rely on pruning for survival, but in a garden, where plants are used for ornamental purposes things are different. Pruning is mainly formative or regenerative. Formative pruning helps to shape and balance a plant in its early stages, whereas regenerative pruning either helps get an overgrown plant back into shape or helps it retain its vigour, and therefore produce more and better flowers or fresh new stems for winter colour. Avoid clipping your shrubs into 'lollipops', unless creating some form of intentional topiary, and look to bring out the natural shape and beauty of each plant.

CLIMBING ROSES

■ Once they have finished flowering, side shoots from the main framework of branches can be cut back to just a couple of buds. Any dead, diseased or spindly growth should be cut out completely and the new, young, flexible shoots tied onto horizontal supports from the base. If there is an old, thick and woody, unproductive stem, it can be removed from the base to stimulate more vigorous growth.

LAWNS

Over the summer your lawn has probably had plenty of wear, so autumn is the time to give your lawn some attention.

■ In early autumn, when the weather is mild, new lawn can be laid using either seed or turf. An autumn-laid lawn will be tougher than one laid in spring, as its root system will be better established.

■ With an existing lawn, give yourself a good workout by scarifying and aerating it. To scarify, use a wire rake to rake hard over the entire lawn to get rid of all the moss and thatch (old dead grass). Aerate the lawn by spiking it with a garden fork to let air and moisture through to promote healthy root growth.

PONDS AND WATER

■ Skim off any fallen leaves from the surface and consider covering it with a net held down with few bricks to keep leaves out altogether.

■ Cut back the foliage of any marginal plants that is falling into the pond, as it's this kind of debris that breaks down in the water and reduces its quality.

MAKING LEAF MOULD

■ If you have enough space, you can easily turn fallen leaves into leaf mould, which makes a great mulch for using around the base of your plants. Simply puncture a few holes in a black bin bag. Rake up the leaves and fill the bag with them and then sprinkle on some water and tie the top. Store the bags in a shady place and the following autumn they will be ready to use.

PROTECTING PLANTS

■ As temperatures start to drop, you will need to think about protecting any exotics and half-hardy plants. Plants such as tree ferns, bananas and palms can be wrapped up using a length of winter fleece or a fleece bag/jacket secured with string or wire. For colder areas, make a simple framework around the plant using chicken wire and stuff it with dry straw for insulation.

■ Any plants grown in pots small enough to move should be transferred to a sheltered corner of the garden, perhaps between the house wall and a boundary for added protection.

WINTER

Winter is the time of year to start planning how you want your garden to look the following year, based on any observations you have made over the previous one. There may be a few routine tasks that need to be done, but really it's an opportunity to do some non-horticultural projects, such as building a compost heap, installing a water butt, tidying up the shed, repainting a wall etc. Winter can be seen as time-out from any essential work in a city garden as, to be honest, most of the jobs can wait until spring.

MAIN JOBS

■ Continue to pick up any fallen leaves, especially on the lawn areas to avoid the development of fungal diseases.
■ When the weather's good, dig over planting areas and incorporate plenty of organic matter into the soil to improve its quality.
■ When the plants are dormant, and as many of them will have dropped their leaves now, you can more easily reach fences, trellis and other garden structures to fix and maintain them.
■ Hire or buy a pressure washer to clean all the hard surfaces, pots and furniture.

BULBS AND PERENNIALS

■ Clear and cut the foliage and debris from any plants that are looking particularly untidy.

TREES, SHRUBS AND CLIMBERS

■ Tough trees, shrubs and roses can be pruned right through the winter, even if the weather is frosty. During the winter it is much easier to identify any dead or diseased wood, which can be cut off and burnt.

LAWNS

■ You can mow the lawn if it puts on any growth during the winter, but keep the mower on a high setting. Winter is the ideal time to get your mower serviced. Its blades should be kept sharp all year round, as it will give a far better and more even cut and the lawn is, therefore, less likely to develop any diseases.

PONDS AND WATER FEATURES

■ If you have a removable pump, unplug it, take it out, clean the filter and store it indoors over winter. If you have fish in your pond make sure to keep an area ice free by floating a plastic ball in it, which will pop out if it freezes over.

SHEDS, STORAGE AND TOOLS
■ Give your shed and any other storage spaces a good clean out. Be ruthless when throwing away anything you don't really need or want.
■ Sharpen and oil all cutting tools such as secateurs and pruners.

COMPOST HEAPS
■ Winter is the ideal time to get your compost heap going. You may have designed it into the garden, but, if not, you can always buy an off-the-peg product such as a rotating bin or build one yourself from old pallets and place it out of sight.
■ You can throw in all your vegetative garden waste (not twiggy stuff unless you shred it first) along with your green kitchen waste (no cooked food or meat as this will encourage rodents). The success of good garden compost, which doesn't smell and has a crumbly texture, is down to layering different types of materials. The material that activates the rotting process and decomposes quickly such as fleshy leaves and grass clippings should be mixed with fibrous material such as the stems of perennials or waste cardboard. Ensure it has enough ventilation and moisture and turn the heap regularly to speed up the decomposition process. Keep seeds and roots of perennial weeds, along with diseased plants, well away.

WORMERIES
■ Wormeries come in kit-form and are great for small quantities of kitchen waste – but not garden waste. They work in layers and the composting worms (which are different to common earthworms) do the job of turning it into garden compost as well as producing a liquid feed that can be diluted for garden use. They do require a bit of looking after, but are fun, organic and interesting for kids. Protect the wormery from heat during the summer, by placing it in the shade. If it is extremely cold in the winter, wrap it in hessian or bubble wrap.

LIST OF SUPPLIERS

NURSERIES

Architectural Plants
Horsham Nursery
Cooks Farm
Nuthurst
Horsham
West Sussex
RH13 6LH
Tel: 01403 891 772
www.architecturalplants.com
Big hardy plants, exotics, bamboos, bananas, palms, ferns, rare evergreen trees and screening plants.

Avon Bulbs
Avon Bulbs Ltd
Burnt House Farm
Mid Lambrook
South Petherton
Somerset
TA13 5HE
Tel: 01460 242 177
www.avonbulbs.co.uk
Bulb specialist with online and mail order service.

Folia Europe
Well End Road
Borehamwood
Hertfordshire
WD6 5NZ
Tel: 020 8953 5827
www.folia-europe.com
Good range of trees, shrubs, topiary and perennials.

Hardy's Cottage Garden Plants
Priory Lane Nursery
Freefolk Priors
Whitchurch
Hampshire
RG28 7NJ
Tel: 01256 896 533
www.hardys-plants.co.uk
More than 1,200 varieties of herbaceous perennials, including many rare and exciting species.

Knoll Gardens
Hampreston
Wimborne
BH21 7ND
Tel: 01202 873 931
www.knollgardens.co.uk
Suppliers of a huge range of wonderful grasses and perennials.

Mulu
c/o The Coach House
Woofferton Grange
Brimfield
Ludlow
Shropshire
SY8 4NP
Tel: 07970 404 409
www.mulu.co.uk
Exotics, unusual and interesting plants pushing the boundaries of hardiness!

Rocket Gardens
Wheal Sara Farm
Horsedowns
Camborne
Cornwall
TR14 0NP
Tel: 01209 831 468
www.rocketgardens.co.uk
Ready grown salad and vegetable plugs. Plants delivered to your door to plant directly into the garden.

STONE

CED Ltd
728 London Road
West Thurrock
Grays
Essex
RM20 3LU
Tel: 01708 867 237
www.ced.ltd.uk
Suppliers of stone paving, aggregates and self binding gravels.

Johnsons Wellfield Quarries Limited
Crosland Hill
Huddersfield
HD4 7AB
Tel: 01484 652 311
www.myersgroup.co.uk
Suppliers of natural Yorkstone quarried from Yorkshire for a wide range of applications.

Silverland Stone
Holloway Hill
Chertsey
Surrey
KT16 0AE
Tel: 01932 569 277
www.silverlandstone.co.uk
Suppliers of stone paving, walling stone, aggregates and self-binding gravels.

Stonemarket
Oxford Road
Ryton on Dunsmore
Warwickshire
CV8 3EJ
Tel: 024 7651 8700
www.stonemarket.co.uk
Imitation and natural stone products for paving and driveways.

TRELLISING

Forest Garden
Unit 291 & 296
Hartlebury Trading Estate
Hartlebury
Worcestershire
DY10 4JB
Tel: 0870 191 9801
www.forestgarden.co.uk
Mainly pressure treated ready made arches, arbours, trellising etc.

Hillhout Ltd
Unit 18 Ellough Industrial Estate
Beccles
Suffolk
NR34 7TD
Tel: 01502 718 091
www.hillhout.com
High quality contemporary wooden trellising, fencing, furniture and garden buildings.

STAINLESS STEEL SOLUTIONS

S3i Ltd
The Old Café
Hudson's Yard
Doncaster Road
Bawtry
Doncaster
DN10 6NX
Tel: 01302 714 513
www.s3i.co.uk
Steel cable trellising and balustrade systems.

TURF

Rolawn Limited
Elvington
York
YO41 4XR
Tel: 0845 604 6050
www.rolawn.co.uk
Garden turf, topsoil and compost.

WATER FEATURES AND PRODUCTS

4Ponds.co.uk
Argham Grange
Grindale
Bridlington
East Yorkshire
YO16 4XZ
www.arghamvillage.co.uk
Suppliers of Bondaglass G4, a liquid applied sealant for making and fixing concrete ponds.

Butyl Products Ltd
11 Radford Crescent
Billericay
Essex
CM12 0DW
Tel: 01277 653 281
www.butylproducts.co.uk
Pond liners in a roll or box welded for a snug fit.

Paul Bromfield Aquatics
Maydencroft Lane
Gosmore
Hitchin
Hertfordshire
SG4 7QD
Tel: 01462 457 399
www.bromfieldaquatics.co.uk
Suppliers of pond plants and pumps for all sizes of ponds.

SafaPond Ltd
Unit 6 Cornel Court
Forest Town
Mansfield
Nottinghamshire
NG19 0NF
Tel: 01623 428 873
www.safapond.com
Modular plastic grids to make ponds of any size or shape safe for children.

Stapeley Water Gardens
London Road
Nantwich
Cheshire
CW5 7LH
Tel: 01270 623 868
www.stapeleywatergardens.com
Suppliers of pond plants, pumps and accessories.

FURNITURE

Dedon (UK supplier)
Leisure Plan
Stansted Mountfitchet
Essex CM24 8HD
Tel: 01279 816 001
www.dedon.co.uk
*Plastic, woven, comfy and stylish
furniture you can leave outside
all year round.*

Elephant
Enterprise D2 Limited
Unit D2 Enterprise Way
Vale Park
Evesham
Worcestershire
WR11 1GS
Tel: 01386 423 760
www.elephantbeanbags.co.uk
*Outdoor beanbags in all shapes,
colours and sizes.*

Gloster Furniture Limited
Collins Drive
Severn Beach
Bristol
BS35 4GG
Tel: 01454 631 950
www.gloster.com
*Range of traditional and
contemporary furniture.*

The Mexican Hammock Company
42 Beauchamp Road
Bristol
BS7 8LQ
Tel: 0117 942 5353
www.hammocks.co.uk
*Excellent hammocks with some
big enough for the whole family!*

STORAGE

Buy Sheds Direct
Tel: 0844 248 9824
www.buyshedsdirect.co.uk
*Environmentally approved sheds
and outside buildings.*

DIY Tools
Taylor Bros (Liverpool) Ltd
www.diytools.co.uk
15-37 Caryl Street
Liverpool
L8 5SQ
Tel: 0151 709 8006
www.diytools.co.uk
*Useful online supplier of tools,
storage and garden buildings etc.*

OUTDOOR OFFICES

The Garden Escape Ltd
Up Beyond
Wye View Lane
Symonds Yat West
Herefordshire
HR9 6B
Tel: 0870 242 7024
www.thegardenescape.co.uk
*A good range of pre-designed
contemporary red cedar timber
and glass buildings or you could
'design your own' and they'll
build it.*

Green Retreats
Coopers Yard
Radclive Road
Gawcott
Buckinghamshire
MK18 4JB
Tel: 01280 824 298
www.greenretreats.co.uk
*Garden rooms and garden
buildings manufactured using
a combination of materials.*

GREEN ROOFS

Enviromat
Q Lawns
Corkway Drove
Hockwold, Thetford
Norfolk IP26 4JR
Tel: 01842 828 266
www.enviromat.co.uk
*Sedum matting on a roll for both
garden and green roof use.*

Greenroof
Blackdown Horticultural
Consultants Limited
Street Ash Nursery
Combe St. Nicholas
Chard
Somerset
TA20 3HZ
Tel: 01460 234 582
www.greenroof.co.uk
*Construction of specialist
greenroof and suppliers of
sedum matting.*

IRRIGATION

Hozelock Limited
Customer Services
Midpoint Park
Minworth
Sutton Coldfield
B76 1AB
Tel: 0870 850 1959
www.hozelock.com
*Easy-to-install hoses, watering
and irrigation systems.*

ACCESSORIES

A.J. Smith and Son (Benfleet) Ltd
242 High Road
Benfleet
Essex
SS7 5LA
Tel: 01268 792 771
www.ajsmith.uk.com
*Timberlocks screws ideal for
decking and sleeper walling, as
they don't need pre-drilling or
countersinking.*

FastenMaster
Olympic Supply Company
The Forge
Wheelers Lane
Linton, Maidstone
Kent
ME17 4BN
Tel: 08452 419 862
www.fastenmaster.com
*All manner of quality fasteners
for every requirement.*

JapanGarden.co.uk
15 Bank Crescent
Ledbury
Herefordshire
HR8 1AA
Tel: 01531 630 041
www.japangarden.co.uk
*Interesting selection of Japanese
furniture, ornament and screens
for the garden.*

Railway Sleepers
Railway Sleeper.com
Cotgrave, Nottingham
NG12 3PU
Tel: 0115 989 0445
www.railwaysleeper.com
*Suppliers of new and used
railway sleepers and other
chunky timber.*

Rawgarden
Bullsbridge Farm
Bumpstead Road
Hempstead
Essex
CB10 2PP
Tel: 0870 609 2398
www.rawgarden.com
*Sail shades, furniture, barbeques,
fire pits etc.*

Specialist Aggregates Ltd
162 Cannock Road
Stafford
ST17 0QJ
Tel: 01785 661 018
www.specialistaggregates.com
*Stones and pebbles to decorative
aggregate finishes such as shells
and recycled glass.*

WORMS

Wiggly Wigglers
Lower Blakemere Farm
Blakemere
Herefordshire
HR2 9PX
Tel: 01981 500 391
www.wigglywigglers.co.uk
*Garden and composting worms,
wormeries, insects and bird feeders.*

Worms Direct UK
Drylands
Ulting
Nr. Maldon
Essex
CM9 6QS
Tel: 01245 381 933
www.wormsdirectuk.co.uk
*All supplies and expert advice on
the different aspects of composting,
worm composting (vermicomposting),
organic recycling and the use
of compost and worm casts in
gardening or horticulture.*

GARDEN DESIGNERS AND LANDSCAPERS

The Association of Professional Landscapers
c/o The Horticultural Trades
Association
19 High Street
Theale
Reading
Berkshire
RG7 5AH
Tel: 0118 930 3132
www.landscaper.org.uk
*Represents many of the UK's
landscape companies.*

Modular Garden
47 Barnsbury Street
London
N1 1TP
Tel: 020 7619 0100
www.modulargarden.com
*High quality gardens, designed
and built for a fixed price.*

Society of Garden Designers
Katepwa House
Ashfield Park Avenue
Ross-on-Wye
Herefordshire
HR9 5AX
Tel: 01989 566 695
www.sgd.org.uk
*The Society of Garden Designers
was established in 1981 and is the
only professional body in the UK
dedicated solely to garden design.*

INDEX

Datura (angel trumpet) 125
see also *Brugmansia*
deadheading 164, 165
decking 24, *25, 31*, 48, *49*, 108
bridges *34*
curved *38*
and drainage *42*, 81
in hot gardens 75
laying 36, 41, *48*
raised platforms *46*
stepping stones *30*
walkways *51*
designing gardens 12, 14–15, 22–3, 24, 28, 63, 107
see also landscaping, hard
Deutzia 165
Dicksonia antarctica (tree fern) *39, 62, 152*, 167
digging 61, 162
dill (*Anethum graveolens*) 102
dining tables and chairs 127, *127*, 128, 129, *137, 154*
dog's-tooth violet see *Erythronium*
dogwoods see *Cornus*
drainage 24, *42*, 79, 81
driveways 108
drought-tolerant plants 52–3, 75, *144*

earthworms 61
Echeveria 75, 145
Echinacea purpurea (coneflower) 95
Echinocacus grusonii 100
edible plants 89, 103, *103*, 147
see also *Tropaeolum majus*
Elodea crispa 121
Eremurus 162
Eriobotrya japonica (loquat) 66, 101, *152*
Eryngium 75
Erysimum cheri (wallflower) 124, 145
Erythronium 'Pagoda' (dog's-tooth violet) 99
Escallonia 123
Eschscholzia californica (Californian poppy) 98
Eucalyptus 19
E. gunnii 163
Eucomis 162
Euonymus alatus 66, 145
Euphorbia (spurge) 146
E. 'Whistleberry Garnet' *88*
E. amygdaloides var. *robbiae* (wood spurge) 96
evening primrose see *Oenothera*
exotic plants 75, 100–101, 117, 167
scented 125

family gardens 30–33
Fargesia murieliae 'Jumbo'

(umbrella bamboo) 66, 101
x *Fatshedera lizei* (tree-ivy) 95
fences/fencing 17, *25*, 68, 87, 110
disguising 46, 149
painting and staining *42, 45, 69*, 110, 148, *151*
fennel (*Foeniculum*) *88*, 102, 122, 146
ferns 72, *93*
tree ferns see *Dicksonia*
fertilisers 161, 162
Festuca glauca 'Elijah Blue' (blue fescue) 97
fig trees 110
fire pits 136, *152*
Foeniculum vulgare 'Purpureum' (bronze fennel) 102
foliage see leaves
forks 60
forsythia 163
foxgloves *93*, 147
French bean (*Phaseolus vulgaris*) 103
fruit trees 103, 110
furniture 114, 128, 153
bringing out from house 157
built-in 129
painting 151, *151*
storing 129
see also benches; dining tables and chairs; seating

*G*alanthus elwesii (snowdrop) 99, 162
games, family 135
Gardenia jasminoides (Cape jasmine) 125
garland lily see *Hedychium*
Garrya elliptica (silk-tassel bush) 94
G. e. 'James Roof' 68
gazebos 66, 75, 105, 111, 157
geranium see *Pelargonium*
Geranium 'Anne Thomson' *146*
giant feather grass see *Stipa*
ginger lily see *Hedychium*
gladioli 162
glass panels *34, 37*
granite blocks 72, 108
grape hyacinth see *Muscari*
grape vine see *Vitis*
grasses, ornamental 18, *45, 49*, 81, *87, 88*, 96, 97, *97*, 146, 162–3, 166
lily grass 145
gravel *43, 51*, 75, 147, 157
grazing lights 132
groundcover plants 59
Guelder rose see *Viburnum opulus*

*H*akonechloa macra 'Aureola' *87*
hammocks 129

hawthorn see *Crataegus prunifolia*
water see *Aponogeton distachyos*
heaters, gas-fired 136
heather 145
Hebe topiaria 30, 92
hedges 18, 165
box *43*, 89
yew 18, 89
Hedychium densifolium 'Assam Orange' (garland *or* ginger lily) 101
Helenium 'Wyndley' 96
Helianthus (sunflower) 99, 123
hellebores 72
herbs 15, 75, 89, 102, 122, *147*
Hesperis matronalis (sweet rocket) 124
Heuchera 58
holiday tips 165
holly 72
honesty see *Lunaria annua*
honey bush see *Melianthus major*
honeysuckle see *Lonicera*
honeywort see *Cerinthe major*
hornbeams 23, *58*
hoses 60
Hosta 72
Hyacinthus (hyacinth) 125
H. 'Woodstock' 125
Hydrangea
H. arborescens 'Annabelle' 37, *86*, 92
H. paniculata 163

*I*mpatiens 145
Indian shot plant see *Canna*
Ipomoea
I. lobata (Spanish flag) 147
I. purpurea 'Purple Haze' (morning glory) 147
Iris
I. reticulata 145
I. r. 'Gordon' 99
I. sibirica 93
irrigation systems 58, *58, 59, 65*
Itea lilicifolia 68
ivies 68, 72, *73*, 94, 110, 145
tree-ivy see *Fatshedera*

*J*apanese anemone see *Anemone hupehensis*; *Anemone* x *hybrida*
Japanese banana see *Musa basjoo*
Japanese maple see *Acer japonica* see *Chaenomeles*
jasmine
Cape see *Gardenia jasminoides*
common see *Jasminum*
star see *Trachelospermum*
Jasminum officinalis (jasmine) 95, 125
Judas tree see *Cercis siliquastrum*

*K*atsura tree see *Cercidiphyllum japonicum*
kitchens, outdoor 136
kumquats 125

*L*actuca sativa (lettuce) 103, 147
ladders 60
lady's mantle see *Alchemilla*
lamb's ear see *Stachys*
landscape fabrics *51, 58, 59*
landscaping *104*, 104–5, *106*, 107
Laurus nobilis (sweet bay) 66, 122
Lavandula (lavender) 72, 75, 122
L. angustifolia 'Hidcote' 125
lawns 75
aerating 167
edges 24, 163
feeding 163, 165
in a box *47, 49*
laying 163, 167
mowing 163, 165, 168
re-turfing 157
scarifying 167
and shaded gardens 72
leaf mould 61, 167
leaves
aromatic 233
clearing up fallen 166
glossy 72
large 65
silver 52, 65, 72, 163
variegated 72
lemon trees 125
lettuces (*Lactuca sativa*) 103, 147
Leucojum (snowflake) 45
levelling sites *13*, 24
lighting 17, 81, 127, *130*, 130–32, *133, 139*
security 132
temporary 155, *155*
lilac 165
lilies
African see *Agapanthus*
arum see *Zantedeschia*
garland see *Hedychium*
ginger see *Hedychium*
scented 125
lily grass 145
lime trees 125
limestone 81, 108
Lonicera (honeysuckle) 95, 165
L. periclymenum 'Serotina' 95, 125
L. x *purpusii* 'Winter Beauty' (shrubby honeysuckle) 125
loquat see *Eriobtrya japonica*
loungers 128
Love-in-a-mist 146
love-lies-bleeding see *Amaranthus*
low-maintenance gardens 52–3
Lunaria annua (honesty) 99, 147
Luzula nivea (snowy woodrush) *62*
Lycopersicon esculentum (tomato) 103

ACKNOWLEDGEMENTS

Many thanks to Jane O'Shea, Laura Herring and Mary Evans at Quadrille Publishing for sharing the same vision and making the writing and picture selection both a pleasurable and creative process (a bit like gardening really!). Thanks to all at Modular Garden and Modular Pro (you know who you are, but too many to mention) who have been involved in the design and/or build of many of the gardens we've included. Thanks to my agents, Luigi Bonomi and Debbie Scheisser. Thanks, also, to all the designers, gardeners, landscapers and lighting specialists whose work is on show, and, of course, to the many photographers whose images we have used. Special thanks to photographer Marianne Majerus for her wonderful pictures and for putting up with the Swifts! Talking of Swifts, love to Cathy, Stanley and Connie who have been great and given me the support and (at least some) peace when it's been needed. Finally, thanks to the Thursday night footy boys for letting me get rid of my pent-up aggression – mainly on them!

2-3 Andrew Lawson/designer Ann Pearce Private garden, Dulwich
4, 70 and **90-1** Marianne Majerus/designer Christopher Bradley-Hole
6 above left, **centre left**, **26-7, 69, 104-5, 115, 137, 152-3, 156-7** and **161** Marianne Majerus/designer Claire Mee
6 above right, **42-5, 82-3** and **112** Marianne Majerus/designer Ann Pearce
6 above centre, **98** and **138-9** Charlotte Rowe Garden Design/Light IQ
6 centre Jerry Harpur/designer Steve Martino
6 centre right Clive Nichols/design Joe Swift/Garden & Security Lighting
6 below left, 10-11, 13-14, 34-7, 69, 86-7, 106, 124, 130-1 and **150 below left** Marianne Majerus/designer Charlotte Rowe
6 below centre Marianne Majerus/designer Alan Smith
6 below right © Andrea Jones/(Barnes garden, London) design by Samantha Woodroofe for Joe Swift and The Plant Room (now Modular Gardens)
15 TIA Digital Limited/Helen Fickling/designer Andy Sturgeon
16 Jerry Harpur/designer Christoph Swinnen
19 and **38-9** © Andrea Jones/Sue Dubois Garden, Islington, London/design by Samantha Woodroofe for Joe Swift and The Plant Room (now Modular Gardens)
20 and **80-1** Andrew Lawson/designer James Aldridge
23 and **133** Jerry Harpur/designer Philip Nash
25 Marianne Majerus/designer Aileen Scoular
29 Jerry Harpur/designer Phoebe Pape
30-1, 32-3, 46-9, 58, 76, 134-5 and **148-9** Marianne Majerus/designer Joe Swift
40-1 © Andrea Jones/design by Samantha Woodroofe for Joe Swift and The Plant Room (now Modular Gardens)
50-1 and **52 above** Nicola Browne/designer Catherine Heatherington
52 right and **53** Helen Fickling/designer Catherine Heatherington
54-5 © Andrea Jones/(Barnes garden, London) design by Samantha Woodroofe for Joe Swift and The Plant Room (now Modular Gardens)
57, 100 and **144** Jerry Harpur/designer Steve Martino
58 left Joe Swift

62 Marianne Majerus/designer James Lee
63-5 and **109** Clive Nichols/design Joe Swift/Thamasin Marsh
66-7 © Andrea Jones (London garden) design by Joe Swift and The Plant Room (now Modular Gardens)
69 above left Clive Nichols/design Joe Swift/Garden & Security Lighting
73, 94 left and **127** © Andrea Jones (London garden)/design Joe Swift and The Plant Room (now Modular Gardens)
74 Marianne Majerus/designed by Lynne Marcus and John Hall
77 left © Andrea Jones/design Mark Gregory/RHS Chelsea Flower Show
77 right Marianne Majerus/designer Natalie Charles
78 and **88-9** Marianne Majerus/designer Andy Sturgeon
85 Jerry Harpur/designer Ulf Nordfjell
93 and **172** Marianne Majerus/designer Ulf Nordfjell
94 right Fab Pics/Thomas Ott
97 Jerry Harpur/designer Christopher Bradley-Hole
103 Marianne Majerus/The Old Vicarage, East Ruston
111 Marianne Majerus/designer Jill Billington
116 Jerry Harpur/designed by Dennis Schrader and Bill Smith
117 © Andrea Jones. Display garden at RHS Wisley
120 Marianne Majerus/designer Jinny Blom
121 above Gap Photos/Howard Rice
121 below © Andrea Jones/designed by Joe Swift and The Plant Room (now Modular Gardens)
122-3 Marianne Majerus/designer Declan Buckley
124 right Marianne Majerus/designer Julie Toll
126 Jerry Harpur/designer Luciano Giubbilei
128-9 and **154** Marianne Majerus/designer Nicola Gammon
140-1 Marianne Majerus/designer Tom Stuart-Smith
143 Marianne Majerus/designer Alastair Howe Architects
146 Marianne Majerus/designer Nicola Lesbirel
147 Marianne Majerus/designer Jane Brockbank
151 Marianne Majerus/design Clifton Nurseries
155 Marianne Majerus/designer George Carter
158-9, 162-9 and **176** Marianne Majerus